RAE PACE ALEXANDER was born in Philadelphia and educated at Boston University and at Bank Street College of Education, New York. She has previously compiled an annotated bibliography of black and bi-racial children's books for the N.A.A.C.P. Her article, "Rigorous Appraisal of Bi-Racial Children's Books," was published by the Council on Interracial Books for Children, Inc. Miss Alexander is at present a candidate for a doctoral degree at Teachers College, Columbia University.

David Parks

JULIUS LESTER was born in St. Louis, Missouri, grew up in Nashville, Tennessee, was graduated from Fisk University, and now lives in New York City with his wife and two children. A frequent reviewer for the New York *Times* Book Review and contributor to national periodicals, Mr. Lester has three adult books, two juveniles, and two record albums to his name. His book *To Be a Slave* was runner-up for the Newbery Prize. He has a regular radio program on WBAI and also teaches at the New School for Social Research.

Through dramatic and moving episodes from their own lives,

eight men and women show what it is to be

Young and Black
in America

Young and Black
in America

compiled by Rae Pace Alexander

introductory notes by Julius Lester

RANDOM HOUSE • NEW YORK

Acknowledgment is gratefully extended to the following for permission to reprint from their works:

David McKay Company, Inc.: From *The Long Shadow of Little Rock,* by Daisy Bates. Copyright © 1962 by Daisy Bates.

The Dial Press: From *Coming of Age in Mississippi,* by Anne Moody. Copyright © 1968 by Anne Moody.

Doubleday & Company, Inc.: From *Off My Chest,* by Jimmy Brown with Myron Cope. Copyright © 1964 by James N. Brown & Myron Cope.

Grove Press, Inc.: From *The Autobiography of Malcolm X,* with the assistance of Alex Haley. Copyright © 1964 by Alex Haley and Malcolm X. Copyright © 1965 by Alex Haley and Betty Shabazz.

Harper & Row, Publishers: From *Black Boy,* by Richard Wright. Copyright 1937, 1942, 1944, 1945 by Richard Wright. From *GI Diary,* by David Parks. Copyright © 1968 by David M. Parks.

The Macmillan Company: From *The Revolt of the Black Athlete,* by Harry Edwards. Copyright © 1969 by The Free Press, a Division of The Macmillan Company.

Library of Congress Catalog Card Number: 70–117005

Manufactured in the United States of America

Designed by Murray M. Herman

Young and Black in America

CONTENTS

CONTENTS

Young and Black in America

Teaching Myself
to Read and Write

Frederick Douglass

Frederick Douglass

Perhaps the most remarkable of the thousands of blacks who escaped from slavery was Frederick Douglass. He was born in February of 1817 or 1818 (he never knew the exact date) in Talbot County, Maryland. Until his escape in 1838, he worked as a slave on plantations and as a house servant in Baltimore.

Upon his escape, he came to New York City where he married Anna Murray, a free black woman he had known in Baltimore. Three years later, Douglass accidentally began what was to be his life's work. He happened to attend a meeting of the Massachusetts Anti-Slavery Society in Nantucket and, taken with the spirit of the gathering, he addressed those present, giving them a vivid account of what life was like for a slave. The Society was so impressed with his speech that he was asked to become an organizer for the anti-slavery movement.

Douglass did so. In the company quite often of William Lloyd Garrison, the leading figure of the Abolitionist movement, he traveled around the country, speaking at public meetings to arouse sentiment against slavery. Along with Garrison and Wendell Phillips, another great anti-slavery leader, Frederick Douglass became one of the greatest orators of the day. With his full beard and impressive head of hair, he was a striking figure on any platform and a natural orator with a command of language given to few.

In 1847 he started his own newspaper, the *North Star*. It was a weekly, devoted to the anti-slavery movement.

Through it, Douglass showed himself to be as skilled a writer as he was a speaker. His editorship of the paper firmly established him as the most important black leader of the time.

His opposition to slavery, however, led him to do more than oppose it in print and from the speaking platform. He was a part of that vast network of hiding places for runaway slaves called the Underground Railroad. His home in Rochester, New York, was one of the last hiding places south of the Canadian border.

Politically, Douglass was, for a long while, a believer in non-violence. However, his faith in this method weakened as he saw the pro-slavery forces of the south grow stronger in the 1850s. When he met John Brown in the mid-1850s, he slowly accepted the fact that slavery might never be abolished except through the use of violence. He and Brown became close friends and Brown tried to persuade him to join the attack on Harpers Ferry. Though Douglass believed in Brown and helped him with money, he refused to join that raid on Harpers Ferry, seeing no possibility of success. When John Brown was captured, Douglass was so implicated in the plot that he had to flee the country to escape arrest.

He went to England, where he had been once before and was well regarded. He returned to the United States on the eve of the Civil War. He spent the war years agitating for the right of blacks to enlist in the Union Army, a right which was eventually granted. After the war he turned his energies to insuring that the rights of the newly freed slaves would be upheld. He was, unfortunately, unsuccessful.

Douglass's stature as a black leader was recognized by

the government. After the war he was appointed to serve as marshal and recorder of deeds of the District of Columbia. In his later years he was, for a brief period, United States Minister to Haiti. He died in 1895.

In the selection below, Douglass describes the difficulties he encountered in learning to read and write—skills which it was illegal for a slave to learn—and the effects, positive and negative, that these newly acquired abilities had on him.

I lived in Master Hugh's family about seven years. During this time, I succeeded in learning to read and write. In accomplishing this, I was compelled to resort to various stratagems. I had no regular teacher. My mistress, who had kindly commenced to instruct me, had, in compliance with the advice and direction of her husband, not only ceased to instruct, but had set her face against my being instructed by any one else.

It is due, however, to my mistress to say of her, that she did not adopt this course of treatment immediately. She at first lacked the depravity indispensable to shutting me up in mental darkness. It was at least necessary for her to have some training in the exercise of irresponsible power, to make her equal to the task of treating me as though I were a brute.

7

My mistress was, as I have said, a kind and tender-hearted woman; and in the simplicity of her soul she commenced, when I first went to live with her, to treat me as she supposed one human being ought to treat another. In entering upon the duties of a slaveholder, she did not seem to perceive that I sustained to her the relation of a mere chattel, and that for her to treat me as a human being was not only wrong, but dangerously so.

Slavery proved as injurious to her as it did to me. When I went there, she was a pious, warm, and tender-hearted woman. There was no sorrow or suffering for which she had not a tear. She had bread for the hungry, clothes for the naked, and comfort for every mourner that came within her reach. Slavery soon proved its ability to divest her of these heavenly qualities. Under its influence, the tender heart became stone, and the lamblike disposition gave way to one of tiger-like fierceness. The first step in her downward course was in her ceasing to instruct me. She now commenced to practise her husband's precepts.

She finally became even more violent in her opposition than her husband himself. She was not satisfied with simply doing as well as he had commanded; she seemed anxious to do better. Nothing seemed to make her more angry than to see me with a newspaper. She seemed to think that here lay the danger. I have had her rush at me with a face made all up of fury, and snatch from me a newspaper, in a manner that fully revealed her apprehension. She was an apt woman; and a little experience soon demonstrated, to her satisfaction, that education and slavery were incompatible with each other.

From this time I was most narrowly watched. If I was in a separate room any considerable length of time, I was sure to be suspected of having a book, and was at once called to give an account of myself. All this, however, was too late. The first step had been taken. Mistress, in teaching me the alphabet, had given me the *inch,* and no precaution could prevent me from taking the *ell.*

The plan which I adopted, and the one by which I was most successful, was that of making friends of all the little white boys whom I met in the street. As many of these as I could, I converted into teachers. With their kindly aid, obtained at different times and in different places, I finally succeeded in learning to read. When I was sent on errands, I always took my book with me, and by going one part of my errand quickly, I found time to get a lesson before my return.

I used also to carry bread with me, enough of which was always in the house, and to which I was always welcome; for I was much better off in this regard than many of the poor white children in our neighborhood. This bread I used to bestow upon the hungry little urchins, who, in return, would give me that more valuable bread of knowledge.

I am strongly tempted to give the names of two or three of those little boys, as a testimonial of the gratitude and affection I bear them; but prudence forbids;—not that it would injure me, but it might embarrass them; for it is almost an unpardonable offence to teach slaves to read in this Christian country. It is enough to say of the dear little fellows, that they lived in Philpot Street, very near Durgin and Bailey's ship-yard.

I used to talk this matter of slavery over with them. I would sometimes say to them, I wished I could be as free as they would be when they got to be men. "You will be free as soon as you are twenty-one, *but I am a slave for life!* Have not I as good a right to be free as you have?"

These words used to trouble them; they would express for me the liveliest sympathy, and console me with the hope that something would occur by which I might be free.

I was now about twelve years old, and the thought of being *a slave for life* began to bear heavily upon my heart. Just about this time, I got hold of a book entitled "The Columbian Orator." Every opportunity I got, I used to read this book. Among much of other interesting matter, I found in it a dialogue between a master and his slave. The slave was represented as having run away from his master three times. The dialogue represented the conversation which took place between them, when the slave was retaken the third time. In this dialogue, the whole argument in behalf of slavery was brought forward by the master, all of which was disposed of by the slave. The slave was made to say some very smart as well as impressive things in reply to his master—things which had the desired though unexpected effect; for the conversation resulted in the voluntary emancipation of the slave on the part of the master.

In the same book, I met with one of Sheridan's mighty speeches on and in behalf of Catholic emancipation. These were choice documents to me. I read them over and over again with unabated interest. They gave tongue to interesting thoughts of my own soul, which had frequently flashed through my mind, and died away for want of utterance. The moral which I gained from the dialogue was the power of truth over the conscience of even a slaveholder. What I got from Sheridan was a bold denunciation of slavery, and a powerful vindication of human rights.

The reading of these documents enabled me to utter my thoughts, and to meet the arguments brought forward to sustain slavery; but while they relieved me of one difficulty, they brought on another even more painful than the one of which I was relieved. The more I read, the more I was led to abhor and detest my enslavers. I could regard them in no other light than a band of successful robbers, who had left their homes, and gone to Africa, and stolen us from our homes, and in a strange land reduced us to slavery. I loathed them as being the meanest as well as the most wicked of men.

As I read and contemplated the subject, behold! that very discontentment which Master Hugh had predicted would follow my learning to read had already come, to torment and sting my soul to unutterable anguish. As I writhed under it, I would at times feel that learning to read had been a curse rather than a blessing. It had given me a view of my wretched condition, without the remedy. It opened my eyes to the horrible pit, but to no ladder upon which to get out. In moments of agony, I envied my fellow-slaves for their stupidity. I have often wished myself a beast. I preferred the condition of the meanest reptile to my own. Any thing, no matter what, to get rid of thinking!

It was this everlasting thinking of my condition that tormented me. There was no getting rid of it. It was pressed upon me by every object within sight or hearing, animate or inanimate. The silver trump of freedom had roused my soul to eternal wakefulness. Freedom now appeared, to disappear no more forever. It was heard in every sound, and seen in every thing. It was ever present to torment me with a sense of my wretched condition. I saw nothing without seeing it. I heard nothing without hearing it, and felt nothing without feeling it. It looked from every star, it smiled in every calm, breathed in every wind, and moved in every storm.

I often found myself regretting my own existence, and wishing myself dead; and but for the hope of being free, I have no doubt but that I should have killed myself, or done something for which I should have been killed. While in this state of mind, I was eager to hear any one speak of slavery. I was a ready listener.

Every little while, I could hear something about the abolitionists. It was some time before I found what the word meant. It was always used in such connections as to make it an interesting word to me. If a slave ran away and succeeded in getting clear, or if a slave killed his master, set fire to a barn, or did any thing very wrong in the mind of a slaveholder, it was spoken of as the fruit of *abolition*. Hearing the word in this connection very often, I set about learning what it meant. The dictionary afforded me little or no help. I found it was "the act of abolishing;" but then I did not know what was to be abolished. Here I was perplexed. I did not dare to ask any one about its meaning, for I was satisfied that it was something they wanted me to know very little about.

After a patient waiting, I got one of our city papers, containing an account of the number of petitions from the north, praying for the abolition of slavery in the

District of Columbia, and of the slave trade between the States. From this time I understood the words *abolition* and *abolitionist,* and always drew near when that word was spoken, expecting to hear something of importance to myself and fellow-slaves. The light broke in upon me by degrees.

I went one day down on the wharf of Mr. Waters; and seeing two Irishmen unloading a scow of stone, I went, unasked, and helped them. When we had finished, one of them came to me and asked me if I were a slave. I told him I was. He asked, "Are ye a slave for life?" I told him that I was. The good Irishman seemed to be deeply affected by the statement. He said to the other that it was a pity so fine a little fellow as myself should be a slave for life. He said it was a shame to hold me. They both advised me to run away to the north; that I should find friends there, and that I should be free.

I pretended not to be interested in what they said, and treated them as if I did not understand them; for I feared they might be treacherous. White men have been known to encourage slaves to escape, and then, to get the reward, catch them and return them to their masters. I was afraid that these seemingly good men might use me so; but I nevertheless remembered their advice, and from that time I resolved to run away. I looked forward to a time at which it would be safe for me to escape. I was too young to think of doing so

14

immediately; besides, I wished to learn how to write, as I might have occasion to write my own pass. I consoled myself with the hope that I should one day find a good chance. Meanwhile, I would learn to write.

The idea as to how I might learn to write was suggested to me by being in Durgin and Bailey's ship-yard, and frequently seeing the ship carpenters, after hewing, and getting a piece of timber ready for use, write on the timber the name of that part of the ship for which it was intended. When a piece of timber was intended for the larboard side, it would be marked thus —"L." When a piece was for the starboard side, it would be marked thus—"S." A piece for the larboard side forward, would be marked thus— "L. F." When a piece was for starboard side forward, it would be marked thus—"S. F." For larboard aft, it would be marked thus—"L. A." For starboard aft, it would be marked thus—"S. A." I soon learned the names of these letters, and for what they were intended when placed upon a piece of timber in the ship-yard. I immediately commenced copying them, and in a short time was able to make the four letters named.

After that, when I met with any boy who I knew could write, I would tell him I could write as well as he.

The next word would be, "I don't believe you. Let me see you try it."

I would then make the letters which I had been so fortunate as to learn, and ask him to beat that. In this way I got a good many lessons in writing, which it is quite possible I should never have gotten in any other way. During this time, my copy-book was the board fence, brick wall, and pavement; my pen and ink was a lump of chalk. With these, I learned mainly how to write. I then commenced and continued copying the Italics in Webster's Spelling Book, until I could make them all without looking on the book.

By this time, my little Master Thomas had gone to school, and learned how to write, and had written over a number of copy-books. These had been brought home, and shown to some of our near neighbors, and then laid aside. My mistress used to go to class meeting at the Wilk Street meetinghouse every Monday afternoon, and leave me to take care of the house. When left thus, I used to spend the time in writing in the spaces left in Master Thomas's copy-book, copying what he had written. I continued to do this until I could write a hand very similar to that of Master Thomas. Thus, after a long, tedious effort for years, I finally succeeded in learning how to write.

Apprentice

Richard Wright

Richard Wright

In 1940, a novel called *Native Son* was published. It was an angry book, representing a black attitude which all but a few whites had unrealistically hoped did not exist. *Native Son* was a loud cry of protest against the lives blacks were forced to lead by white America. The novel remains one of the great works of American literature and made its author one of the most important writers in this country's history.

The anger of Richard Wright came from the hard realities of his everyday existence. Born in 1908 in Jackson, Mississippi, he grew up in a society where lynchings and physical brutality were commonplace. In Mississippi it was literally true that a black man had no rights which a white man had to respect. Under such conditions, blacks developed pretense to the height of a fine art, because survival depended upon hiding one's true feelings and thoughts. They learned to smile when they were angry, laugh when they felt like crying, and dance and sing when they wanted to commit murder.

Richard Wright, however, found it impossible to pretend to something he didn't feel. He was angry and could not hide that anger. If he had not left Mississippi as a young man, his anger would have led him to death or prison. There were no other ends for an angry black, in Mississippi or practically anywhere else in America.

Wright left Mississippi and went to Chicago, Illinois, where he found life a little less brutal, but otherwise no different. Even after the publication of *Native Son* and his subsequent fame, life continued to be a brutalizing experience for him. He was famous and he was black. He reaped few of the rewards of success and all of the brutalities of being black in white America.

In the late 1940s Wright moved to Paris with his wife and daughter. There he remained and continued to write. His major works include: *Uncle Tom's Children* (1938), a collection of short stories; *Black Boy* (1945); *Black Power* (1954), a book about the African nation of Ghana on the eve of independence; *Pagan Spain* (1957); *White Man, Listen!* (1957); and *The Long Dream* (1958). In the fall of 1960 he died.

More than any other black writer, Richard Wright described—with numbing realism—the brutal effects on the mind and emotions of being black in America. In the history of literature, there are few books more painful to read than *Black Boy*—Wright's account of his childhood in Mississippi. In this book, he makes the reader feel what it is like to have a society try to make one's skin into a concentration camp. In the remarkable passage reprinted here, all of it is there—the constant threat of physical and psychological violence, the black survival techniques, the pain, the constant effort by whites to dehumanize blacks. It is amazing that Richard Wright refused to bow his head. He survived by fighting.

———————◆———————

I held a series of petty jobs for short periods, quitting some to work elsewhere, being driven off others because of my attitude, my speech, the look in my eyes. I was no nearer than ever to my goal of saving enough money to leave. At times I doubted if I could ever do it.

One jobless morning I went to my old classmate, Griggs, who worked for a Capitol Street jeweler. He was washing the windows of the store when I came upon him.

"Do you know where I can find a job?" I asked.

He looked at me with scorn.

"Yes, I know where you can find a job," he said, laughing.

"Where?"

"But I wonder if you can hold it," he said.

"What do you mean?" I asked. "Where's the job?"

"Take your time," he said. "You know, Dick, I know you. You've been trying to hold a job all summer, and you can't. Why? Because you're impatient. That's your big fault."

I said nothing, because he was repeating what I had already heard him say. He lit a cigarette and blew out smoke leisurely.

"Well," I said, egging him on to speak.

"I wish to hell I could talk to you," he said.

"I think I know what you want to tell me," I said.

He clapped me on the shoulder; his face was full of fear, hate, concern for me.

"Do you want to get killed?" he asked me.

"Hell, no!"

"Then, for God's sake, learn how to live in the South!"

"What do you mean?" I demanded. "Let white people tell me that. Why should you?"

"See?" he said triumphantly, pointing his finger at me. "There it is, *now*! It's in your face. You won't let people tell you things. You rush too much. I'm trying to help you and you won't let me." He paused and looked about; the streets were filled with white people. He spoke to me in a low, full tone. "Dick, look, you're black, black, *black*, see? Can't you understand that?"

"Sure, I understand it," I said.

"You don't act a damn bit like it," he spat.

He then reeled off an account of my actions on every job I had held that summer.

"How did you know that?" I asked.

"White people make it their business to watch niggers," he explained. "And they pass the word around.

22

Now, my boss is a Yankee and he tells me things. You're marked already."

Could I believe him? Was it true? How could I ever learn this strange world of white people?

"Then tell me how must I act?" I asked humbly. "I just want to make enough money to leave."

"Wait and I'll tell you," he said.

At that moment a woman and two men stepped from the jewelry store; I moved to one side to let them pass, my mind intent upon Griggs's words. Suddenly Griggs reached for my arm and jerked me violently, sending me stumbling three or four feet across the pavement. I whirled.

"What's the matter with you?" I asked.

Griggs glared at me, then laughed.

"I'm teaching you how to get out of white people's way," he said.

I looked at the people who had come out of the store; yes, they were *white*, but I had not noticed it.

"Do you see what I mean?" he asked. "White people want you out of their way." He pronounced the words slowly so that they would sink into my mind.

"I know what you mean," I breathed.

"Dick, I'm treating you like a brother," he said. "You act around white people as if you didn't know that they were white. And they *see* it."

"Oh, Christ, I can't be a slave," I said hopelessly.

"But you've got to eat," he said.

"Yes, I got to eat."

"Then start acting like it," he hammered at me, pounding his fist in his palm. "When you're in front of white people, *think* before you act, *think* before you speak. Your way of doing things is all right among *our* people, but not for *white* people. They won't stand for it."

I stared bleakly into the morning sun. I was nearing my seventeenth birthday and I was wondering if I would ever be free of this plague. What Griggs was saying was true, but it was simply utterly impossible for me to calculate, to scheme, to act, to plot all the time. I would remember to dissemble for short periods, then I would forget and act straight and human again, not with the desire to harm anybody, but merely forgetting the artificial status of race and class. It was the same with whites as with blacks; it was my way with everybody. I sighed, looking at the glittering diamonds in the store window, the rings and the neat rows of golden watches.

"I guess you're right," I said at last. "I've got to watch myself, break myself . . ."

"No," he said quickly, feeling guilty now. Someone —a white man—went into the store and we paused in our talk. "You know, Dick, you may think I'm an Uncle Tom, but I'm not. I hate these white people, hate 'em with all my heart. But I can't show it; if I did, they'd kill me." He paused and looked around to see if

24

there were any white people within hearing distance. "Once I heard an old drunk nigger say:

> *All these white folks dressed so fine*
> *Their ass-holes smell just like mine . . ."*

I laughed uneasily, looking at the white faces that passed me. But Griggs, when he laughed, covered his mouth with his hand and bent at the knees, a gesture which was unconsciously meant to conceal his excessive joy in the presence of whites.

"That's how I feel about 'em," he said proudly after he had finished his spasm of glee. He grew sober. "There's an optical company upstairs and the boss is a Yankee from Illinois. Now, he wants a boy to work all day in summer, mornings and evenings in winter. He wants to break a colored boy into the optical trade. You know algebra and you're just cut out for the work. I'll tell Mr. Crane about you and I'll get in touch with you."

"Do you suppose I could see him now?" I asked.

"For God's sake, take your *time!*" he thundered at me.

"Maybe that's what's wrong with Negroes," I said. "They take too much time."

I laughed, but he was disturbed. I thanked him and left. For a week I did not hear from him and I gave up hope. Then one afternoon Griggs came to my house.

"It looks like you've got a job," he said. "You're going to have a chance to learn a trade. But remember to keep your head. Remember you're black. You start tomorrow."

"What will I get?"

"Five dollars a week to start with; they'll raise you if they like you," he explained.

My hopes soared. Things were not quite so bad, after all. I would have a chance to learn a trade. And I need not give up school. I told him that I would take the job, that I would be humble.

"You'll be working for a Yankee and you ought to get along," he said.

The next morning I was outside the office of the optical company long before it opened. I was reminding myself that I must be polite, must think before I spoke, must think before I acted, must say "yes sir, no sir," that I must so conduct myself that white people would not think that I thought I was as good as they. Suddenly a white man came up to me.

"What do you want?" he asked me.

"I'm reporting for a job, sir," I said.

"O.K. Come on."

I followed him up a flight of steps and he unlocked the door of the office. I was a little tense, but the young white man's manner put me at ease and I sat and held my hat in my hand. A white girl came and began punching the typewriter. Soon another white man, thin and gray, entered and went into the rear room. Finally a tall, red-faced white man arrived, shot me a quick glance and sat at his desk. His brisk manner branded him a Yankee.

"You're the new boy, eh?"

"Yes, sir."

"Let me get my mail out of the way and I'll talk with you," he said pleasantly.

"Yes, sir."

I even pitched my voice to a low plane, trying to rob it of any suggestion or overtone of aggressiveness.

Half an hour later Mr. Crane called me to his desk and questioned me closely about my schooling, about how much mathematics I had had. He seemed pleased when I told him that I had had two years of algebra.

"How would you like to learn this trade?" he asked.

"I'd like it fine, sir. I'd like nothing better," I said.

He told me that he wanted to train a Negro boy in the optical trade; he wanted to help him, guide him. I tried to answer in a way that would let him know that I would try to be worthy of what he was doing. He took me to the stenographer and said:

"This is Richard. He's going to be with us."

He then led me into the rear room of the office, which turned out to be a tiny factory filled with many strange machines smeared with red dust.

"Reynolds," he said to a young white man, "this is Richard."

"What you saying there, boy!" Reynolds grinned and boomed at me.

Mr. Crane took me to the older man.

"Pease, this is Richard, who'll work with us."

Pease looked at me and nodded. Mr. Crane then held forth to the two white men about my duties: he told them to break me in gradually to the workings of the shop, to instruct me in the mechanics of grinding and polishing lenses. They nodded their assent.

"Now, boy, let's see how clean you can get this place," Mr. Crane said.

"Yes, sir."

I swept, mopped, dusted, and soon had the office and the shop clean. In the afternoons, when I had caught up with my work, I ran errands. In an idle moment I would stand and watch the two white men grinding lenses on the machines. They said nothing to me and I said nothing to them. The first day passed, the second, the third, a week passed and I received my five dollars. A month passed. But I was not learning anything and nobody had volunteered to help me. One afternoon I walked up to Reynolds and asked him to tell me about the work.

"What are you trying to do, get smart, nigger?" he asked me.

"No, sir," I said.

I was baffled. Perhaps he just did not want to help me. I went to Pease, reminding him that the boss had said that I was to be given a chance to learn the trade.

"Nigger, you think you're white, don't you?"

"No, sir."

"You're acting mighty like it," he said.

"I was only doing what the boss told me to do," I said.

Pease shook his fist in my face.

"This is a *white* man's work around here," he said.

From then on they changed toward me: they said good morning no more. When I was just a bit slow in performing some duty, I was called a lazy black son-ofabitch. I kept silent, striving to offer no excuse for worsening of relations. But one day Reynolds called me to his machine.

"Nigger, you think you'll ever amount to anything?" he asked in a slow, sadistic voice.

"I don't know, sir," I answered, turning my head away.

"What do niggers think about?" he asked.

"I don't know, sir," I said, my head still averted.

"If I was a nigger, I'd kill myself," he said.

I said nothing. I was angry.

"You know why?" he asked.

I still said nothing.

"But I don't reckon niggers mind being niggers," he said suddenly and laughed.

I ignored him. Mr. Pease was watching me closely; then I saw them exchange glances. My job was not leading to what Mr. Crane had said it would. I had been humble, and now I was reaping the wages of humility.

"Come here, boy," Pease said.

I walked to his bench.

"You didn't like what Reynolds just said, did you?" he asked.

"Oh, it's all right," I said smiling.

"You didn't like it. I could see it on your face," he said.

I stared at him and backed away.

"Did you ever get into any trouble?" he asked.

"No, sir."

"What would you do if you got into trouble?"

"I don't know, sir."

"Well, watch yourself and don't get into trouble," he warned.

I wanted to report these clashes to Mr. Crane, but the thought of what Pease or Reynolds would do to me if they learned that I had "snitched" stopped me. I worked through the days and tried to hide my resentment under a nervous, cryptic smile.

The climax came at noon one summer day. Pease called me to his workbench; to get to him I had to go between two narrow benches and stand with my back against a wall.

"Richard, I want to ask you something," Pease began pleasantly, not looking up from his work.

"Yes, sir."

Reynolds came over and stood blocking the narrow passage between the benches; he folded his arms and stared at me solemnly. I looked from one to the other, sensing trouble. Pease looked up and spoke slowly, so there would be no possibility of my not understanding.

"Richard, Reynolds here tells me that you called me Pease," he said.

I stiffened. A void opened up in me. I knew that this was the showdown.

He meant that I had failed to call him Mr. Pease. I looked at Reynolds; he was gripping a steel bar in his hand. I opened my mouth to speak, to protest, to assure Pease that I had never called him simply *Pease*, and that I had never had any intention of doing so, when Reynolds grabbed me by the collar, ramming my head against a wall.

"Now, be careful, nigger," snarled Reynolds, baring his teeth. "I heard you call 'im *Pease*. And if you say you didn't, you're calling me a liar, see?" He waved the steel bar threateningly.

If I had said: No, sir, Mr. Pease, I never called you *Pease*, I would by inference have been calling Reynolds a liar; and if I had said: Yes, sir, Mr. Pease, I called you *Pease*, I would have been pleading guilty to the worst insult that a Negro can offer to a southern white man. I stood trying to think of a neutral

31

course that would resolve this quickly risen nightmare, but my tongue would not move.

"Richard, I asked you a question!" Pease said. Anger was creeping into his voice.

"I don't remembering calling you *Pease*, Mr. Pease," I said cautiously. "And if I did, I sure didn't mean . . ."

"You black sonofabitch! You called me *Pease*, then!" he spat, rising and slapping me till I bent sideways over a bench.

Reynolds was up on top of me demanding:

"Didn't you call him *Pease?* If you say you didn't, I'll rip your gut string loose with this f--k--g bar, you black granny dodger! You can't call a white man a liar and get away with it!"

I wilted. I begged them not to hit me. I knew what they wanted. They wanted me to leave the job.

"I'll leave," I promised. "I'll leave right now!"

They gave me a minute to get out of the factory, and warned me not to show up again or tell the boss. Reynolds loosened his hand on my collar and I ducked out of the room. I did not see Mr. Crane or the stenographer in the office. Pease and Reynolds had so timed it that Mr. Crane and the stenographer would be out when they turned on the terror. I went to the street and waited for the boss to return. I saw Griggs wiping glass shelves in the jewelry store and I beckoned to him. He came out and I told him what had happened.

"Then what are you standing there like a fool for?" he demanded. "Won't you ever learn? Get home! They might come down!"

I walked down Capitol Street feeling that the sidewalk was unreal, that I was unreal, that the people were unreal, yet expecting somebody to demand to know what right I had to be on the streets. My wound went deep; I felt that I had been slapped out of the human race. When I reached home, I did not tell the family what had happened; I merely told them that I had quit, that I was not making enough money, that I was seeking another job.

That night Griggs came to my house; we went for a walk.

"You got a goddamn tough break," he said.

"Can you say it was my fault?" I asked.

He shook his head.

"Well, what about your goddamn philosophy of meekness?" I asked him bitterly.

"These things just happen," he said, shrugging.

"They owe me money," I said.

"That's what I came about," he said. "Mr. Crane wants you to come in at ten in the morning. Ten sharp, now, mind you, because he'll be there and those guys won't gang up on you again."

The next morning at ten I crept up the stairs and peered into the office of the optical shop to make sure that Mr. Crane was in. He was at his desk. Pease and

Reynolds were at their machines in the rear.

"Come in, Richard," Mr. Crane said.

I pulled off my hat and walked into the office; I stood before him.

"Sit down," he said.

I sat. He stared at me and shook his head.

"Tell me, what happened?"

An impulse to speak rose in me and died with the realization that I was facing a wall that I would never breach. I tried to speak several times and could make no sounds. I grew tense and tears burnt my cheeks.

"Now, just keep control of yourself," Mr. Crane said.

I clenched my fists and managed to talk.

"I tried to do my best here," I said.

"I believe you," he said. "But I want to know what happened. Which one bothered you?"

"Both of 'em," I said.

Reynolds came running to the door and I rose. Mr. Crane jumped to his feet.

"Get back in there," he told Reynolds.

"That nigger's lying!" Reynolds said. "I'll kill 'im if he lies on me!"

"Get back in there or get out," Mr. Crane said.

Reynolds backed away, keeping his eyes on me.

"Go ahead," Mr. Crane said. "Tell me what happened."

Then again I could not speak. What could I accomplish by telling him? I was black; I lived in the South. I would never learn to operate those machines as long as those two white men in there stood by them. Anger and fear welled in me as I felt what I had missed; I leaned forward and clapped my hands to my face.

"No, no, now," Mr. Crane said. "Keep control of yourself. No matter what happens, keep control . . ."

"I know," I said in a voice not my own. "There's no use of my saying anything."

"Do you want to work here?" he asked me.

I looked at the white faces of Pease and Reynolds; I imagined their waylaying me, killing me. I was remembering what had happened to Ned's brother.

"No, sir," I breathed.

"Why?"

"I'm scared," I said. "They would kill me."

Mr. Crane turned and called Pease and Reynolds into the office.

"Now, tell me which one bothered you. Don't be afraid. Nobody's going to hurt you," Mr. Crane said.

I stared ahead of me and did not answer. He waved the men inside. The white stenographer looked at me with wide eyes and I felt drenched in shame, naked to my soul. The whole of my being felt violated, and I knew that my own fear had helped to violate it. I was breathing hard and struggling to master my feelings.

"Can I get my money, sir?" I asked at last.

"Just sit a minute and take hold of yourself," he said.

I waited and my roused senses grew slowly calm.

"I'm awfully sorry about this," he said.

"I had hoped for a lot from this job," I said. "I'd wanted to go to school, to college . . ."

"I know," he said. "But what are you going to do now?"

My eyes traveled over the office, but I was not seeing.

"I'm going away," I said.

"What do you mean?"

"I'm going to get out of the South," I breathed.

"Maybe that's best," he said. "I'm from Illinois. Even for me, it's hard here. I can do just so much."

He handed me my money, more than I had earned for the week. I thanked him and rose to leave. He rose. I went into the hallway and he followed me. He reached out his hand.

"It's tough for you down here," he said.

I barely touched his hand. I walked swiftly down the hall, fighting against crying again. I ran down the steps, then paused and looked back up. He was standing at the head of the stairs, shaking his head. I went into the sunshine and walked home like a blind man.

How My Mother Died

Daisy Bates

Daisy Bates

On May 17, 1954, the United States Supreme Court ruled that segregation in the public schools was unconstitutional. This historic ruling struck at the very core of the social structure of the South and it was to be expected that many cities and states would be unwilling to put it into practice. The first big confrontation came in Little Rock, Arkansas, in the fall of 1957.

Nine black students were to enter all-white Central High School. A few days before school was to open, Orval Faubus, then governor of Arkansas, ordered the National Guard to surround the school. He reasoned that violence would occur when the nine blacks tried to enter the school. However, instead of ordering the National Guard to stop any violence which might occur, he ordered the Guard to keep the blacks out of the school. This was the first open defiance of the Supreme Court decision by a top state official.

The nine black students, their parents and advisers, had a difficult decision to make. Should the students still try to enter Central High? It was decided that they should. When the day came mobs of whites lined the sidewalk and filled the street in front of the school. The National Guard blocked the entrances, pointed bayonets at the black students, and refused to escort them to safety through the crowd of whites. As the students tried to make their way through the mob, they were spat upon and beaten.

The central figure in this drama was Mrs. Daisy Bates, state president of the National Association for the Advancement of Colored People. Born and raised in the small town of Huttig, Arkansas, Daisy Lee Gatson married when she was eighteen years old and with her husband, L. C. Bates, moved to Little Rock. There, they decided to assume the ownership of a weekly newspaper, the *State Press*. Together, they slowly made the paper into the voice of blacks in Arkansas, protesting police brutality, the lack of equal rights in housing, in jobs, and in the courtroom.

In 1952 Mrs. Bates was elected president of the Arkansas State Conference of the NAACP. The NAACP had taken the lead in the fight for the desegregation of schools. It was involved in many court cases throughout the South, trying to make sure that the 1954 ruling was put into practice. Such an effort required not only the skills of lawyers, but also the commitment of many anonymous people, like Mrs. Bates, who were responsible for building strong organizations on the local level to prepare for the day when desegregation came. Just how important such preparation was did not become clear, however, until the confrontation around Central High.

When the governor said that there would be no desegregation, the blacks of Little Rock could either bow their heads or fight. Much of the burden for the decision was carried by Mrs. Bates, as a leader of the black community. The decision to fight placed the lives of all who were involved in great danger. Without the kind of leadership and courage shown by Mrs. Bates, the ordeal could not have been endured.

Mrs. Bates's life was constantly threatened and for many months she did not leave her home without carrying a gun, or go to bed at night without armed guards posted outside her home. The newspaper which she and her husband had built was forced out of business by whites. Yet Mrs. Bates and the blacks of Little Rock persevered. Her book, *The Long Shadow of Little Rock,* is more than her personal story. It is the story of countless blacks who, in extraordinary times, have had to show extraordinary courage.

In the excerpt below, Mrs. Bates tells of her childhood, the murder of her mother, the death of her foster father, and the profound effect his dying words had on her adult life.

———————◆———————

I was born Daisy Lee Gatson in the little sawmill town of Huttig, in southern Arkansas. The owners of the mill ruled the town. Huttig might have been called a sawmill plantation, for everyone worked for the mill, lived in houses owned by the mill, and traded at the general store run by the mill.

The hard, red clay streets of the town were mostly unnamed. Main Street, the widest and longest street in town, and the muddiest after a rain, was the site of our business square. It consisted of four one-story buildings which housed a commissary and meat market, a post office, an ice cream parlor, and a movie house. Main Street also divided "White Town" from "Negra Town." However, the physical appearance of the two areas provided a more definite means of distinction.

The Negro citizens of Huttig were housed in rarely painted, drab red "shotgun" houses, so named because one could stand in the front yard and look straight through the front and back doors into the back yard. The Negro community was also provided with two church buildings of the same drab red exterior, although kept spotless inside by the Sisters of the church, and a two-room schoolhouse equipped with a potbellied stove that never quite succeeded in keeping it warm.

On the other side of Main Street were white bungalows, white steepled churches and a white spacious school with a big lawn. Although the relations between Negro and white were cordial, the tone of the community, as indicated by outward appearances, was of the "Old South" tradition.

As I grew up in this town, I knew I was a Negro, but I did not really understand what that meant until I was seven years old. My parents, as do most Negro parents, protected me as long as possible from the inevitable insult and humiliation that is, in the South, a part of being "colored."

I was a proud and happy child—all hair and legs, my cousin Early B. used to say—and an only child, although not blessed with the privilege of having my way. One afternoon, shortly after my seventh birthday, my mother called me in from play.

"I'm not feeling well," she said. "You'll have to go to the market to get the meat for dinner."

I was thrilled with such an important errand. I put on one of my prettiest dresses and my mother brushed my hair. She gave me a dollar and instructions to get a pound of center-cut pork chops. I skipped happily all the way to the market.

When I entered the market, there were several white adults waiting to be served. When the butcher had finished with them, I gave him my order. More white adults entered. The butcher turned from me and took their orders. I was a little annoyed but felt since they were grownups it was all right. While he was waiting on the adults, a little white girl came in and we talked while we waited.

The butcher finished with the adults, looked down at us and asked, "What do you want, little girl?" I smiled and said, "I told you before, a pound of center-cut pork chops." He snarled, "I'm not talking to you," and again asked the white girl what she wanted. She also wanted a pound of center-cut pork chops.

"Please may I have my meat?" I said, as the little girl left. The butcher took my dollar from the counter, reached into the showcase, got a handful of fat chops and wrapped them up. Thrusting the package at me, he said, "Niggers have to wait 'til I wait on the white people. Now take your meat and get out of here!" I ran all the way home crying.

When I reached the house, my mother asked what had happened. I started pulling her toward the door, telling her what the butcher had said. I opened the meat and showed it to her. "It's fat, Mother. Let's take it back."

"Oh, Lord, I knew I shouldn't have sent her. Stop crying now, the meat isn't so bad."

"But it is. Why can't we take it back?"

"Go on out on the porch and wait for Daddy." As she turned from me, her eyes were filling with tears.

When I saw Daddy approaching, I ran to him, crying. He lifted me in his arms and smiled. "Now, what's wrong?" When I told him, his smile faded.

"And if we don't hurry, the market will be closed," I finished.

"We'll talk about it after dinner, sweetheart." I could feel his muscles tighten as he carried me into the house.

Dinner was distressingly silent. Afterward my parents went into the bedroom and talked. My mother came out and told me my father wanted to see me. I ran into the bedroom. Daddy sat there, looking at me for a long time. Several times he tried to speak, but the words just wouldn't come. I stood there, looking at him and wondering why he was acting so strangely. Finally he stood up and the words began tumbling from him. Much of what he said I did not understand.

44

To my seven-year-old mind he explained as best he could that a Negro had no rights that a white man respected.

He dropped to his knees in front of me, placed his hands on my shoulders, and began shaking me and shouting.

"Can't you understand what I've been saying?" he demanded. "There's nothing I can do! If I went down to the market I would only cause trouble for my family."

As I looked at my daddy sitting by me and with tears in his eyes, I blurted out innocently, "Daddy, are you afraid?"

He sprang to his feet in an anger I had never seen before. "Hell, no! I'm not afraid for myself, I'm not afraid to die. I could go down to that market and tear him limb from limb with my bare hands, but I am afraid for you and your mother."

That night when I knelt to pray, instead of my usual prayers, I found myself praying that the butcher would die. After that night we never mentioned him again.

Shortly after my eighth birthday I was playing with other children on a neighbor's steps. An older boy, whom I didn't happen to like, came up and began pulling my braids. I said I was going home. The boy said, "You always act so uppity. If you knew what happened to your mother, you wouldn't act so stuck up."

"Nothing's wrong with my mother," I retorted. "I just left her."

"I'm talking about your *real* mother, the one the white man took out and killed."

"That's a story and you're a mean and nasty old boy!" I began to cry.

"It ain't. I heard my folks talking about it."

Just then the mother of one of my playmates came out on the porch and yelled at the boy. "Shut up! You talk too much. I'm going to tell your mother, and you'll get the beating of your life.

"Honey," she said to me, "don't believe nothing that no-good boy says." Still, I wondered what if he was telling me the truth?

At dinner that evening I looked intently at my parents, all the while trying to decide whether I looked like them. I could see no resemblance or likeness to myself in either of them. I remembered many little things, like the day Mother was talking to a salesman when I came in. He glanced at me, then turned to my mother.

"Have you heard from her father?" he had asked her.

When my mother said she hadn't, the salesman nodded toward me. "Does she know?"

"We haven't told her," my mother had said.

During the next few weeks I kept so much to myself that my parents decided that I must be sick. So
I was "dosed" up with little pink pills. My cousin
Early B. came to visit us. He was several years older
than I, but I was always glad to see him because he
protected me from the boys who liked to taunt and
tease me.

One afternoon as we walked along the millpond,
I asked Early B. to tell me about my mother. He
looked at me puzzled.

"Your mother?" he said guardedly, and pointed in
the direction of my house. We could see her sitting
on the porch.

"No. I mean my *real* mother."

"You know?"

"Yes."

"Everything?"

"Well, almost."

"Who told you? I'll knock his block off! Have you
told your mamma and papa?"

"No."

We walked on in silence until we stood on the
bank that divided the millpond from the town's fishing hole. Large logs floated in the water. The smell
of fresh-cut lumber mixed with the odor of dead fish.
As we stood there, Early B. told me of my parents.

"One night when you were a baby and your daddy
was working nights at the mill, a man went to your

house and told your mother that your daddy had been hurt. She rushed out, leaving you alone, but she met a neighbor and asked her to listen out for you while she went to see about your daddy.

"When your daddy got home the next morning, he found you alone. He went around asking the neighbors if they had seen your mother. The neighbor your mother had asked to look after you told him what happened the night before—that she saw a man who looked like he was colored, although she didn't get a good look at him because he was walking in front of your mother.

"The news spread fast around town that your mother couldn't be found. Later in the morning, some people out fishing found her body."

Early B. stopped talking and sat down on the pond bank. I stood over him, looking into the dark, muddy water.

"Where did they find her?" I asked.

After a long silence Early B. pointed at the water and said, "Right down there. She was half in and half out."

"Who did it?"

"Well," he answered, "there was a lot of talk from the cooks and cleaning women who worked in 'white town' about what they had heard over there. They said that three white men did it."

"What happened to my father?"

"He was so hurt, he left you with the people who have you now, his best friends. He left town. Nobody has heard from him since."

"What did my real parents look like?"

"They were young. Your daddy was as light as a lot of white people. Your mother was very pretty—dark brown, with long black hair."

Early B.'s friends came along and he wandered off with them. I sat there looking into the dark waters, vowing that some day I would get the men who killed my mother. I did not realize that the afternoon had turned into evening and darkness had closed in around me until someone sitting beside me whispered, "It's time to go home, darling." I turned and saw my daddy sitting beside me. He reached out in the darkness and took my hand.

"How long have you known?" he asked.

"A long time," I said.

He lifted me tenderly in his arms and carried me home.

The next morning I had a high temperature. I remember the neighbors coming in, talking in quiet tones. That afternoon a playmate brought me a little box holding three guinea pigs. At first I thought they were rats. Knowing my mother's fear of rats, I hid the box in my bed.

That night the Church Sisters, who met each week at the church or at the home of some sick person to pray, gathered at our home. They knelt around my bed and prayed for my soul. I noticed the fat knees of one praying lady. It gave me an idea I couldn't resist. I eased the box to the floor and released the guinea pigs. One of them ran across the fat lady's leg. Unable to lift her weight up on the chair beside her, she lumbered around the room, screaming hysterically. The other ladies, managing to keep a few paces ahead of her, joined in the wild demonstration.

Above the hubbub I heard my mother's voice sternly demanding to know where the creatures came from. Helpless with laughter, I could not reply. The guinea pigs broke up the prayer meeting and I got my behind properly spanked. The ladies, although convinced that I certainly needed prayer, decided to do their praying for me elsewhere.

In Arkansas, even in the red clay soil of a mill town, flowers grow without any encouragement at all. Everyone's yard had some sort of flowering bush or plant all spring and summer. And in this town of Huttig, where there was so little beauty, I passionately loved all blooming things. In the woods I hunted out the first of the cowslips and spring beauties, and from open fields, the last of the Indian paintbrush. I was always bringing home bouquets.

All of the neighbors knew that the flowers in our yard were my garden, not Mother's. I had no favorites and delighted at each flower in its season. When the last roses and zinnias had died, I knew in a few short months the old lilac bush would start budding, for winter in Arkansas is short-lived. But this year was different. One morning I was out before breakfast looking for flowers to pick. All I found was a single red rose, the dew still wet on it. I can close my eyes today and see exactly how it looked. Unaccountably I turned, leaving it on its stalk, and walked into the house crying.

My mother met me at the door and I saw her face cloud with anxiety. What was the trouble? "All the other flowers were dead," I sobbed, "and my rose will die, too."

That night I heard her say to Daddy, "I can't understand that child, crying over a dying flower." Then I heard my daddy say, "Let her be. It just takes time."

My family had not spoken to me of my real mother since that day the ladies came to pray for me.

Later in the fall, on a Saturday afternoon, my father and I took a walk in the woods. It was a brisk day. Daddy thought we might find some ripe persimmons. Also, some black walnuts might have fallen from a big old tree he knew about. We walked along sniffing the air, sharp with the smell of pine needles, then came out in an open stretch in sight of the persimmon grove. I was always happy on these excursions with Daddy. I guess it was just the feeling that I couldn't be happy now, couldn't let myself be, that made me ask the question.

"Daddy, who killed my mother? Why did they kill her?"

We walked on a little way in silence. Then he pointed to some flat rocks on a slope, and we made our way there and rested. The persimmons and walnuts were forgotten. He began in tones so soft I could barely hear the words.

He told me of the timeworn lust of the white man for the Negro woman—which strikes at the heart of every Negro man in the South. I don't remember a time when this man I called my father didn't talk to me almost as if I were an adult. Even so, this was a difficult concept to explain to an eight-year-old girl; but he spoke plainly, in simple words I could understand. He wanted me to realize that my mother wouldn't have died if it hadn't been for her race— as well as her beauty, her pride, her love for my father.

"Your mother was not the kind to submit," he said, "so they took her." His voice grew bitter. "They say that three white men did it. There was some talk about who they were, but no one knew for sure, and the sheriff's office did little to find out."

He said some other things about the way the Negro is treated in the South, but my mind had stopped, fastening on those three white men and what they had done. They had killed my mother.

When we walked out of the woods, my daddy looked tired and broken. He took my hand and we walked home in silence.

Dolls, games, even my once-beloved fishing, held little interest for me after that. Young as I was, strange as it may seem, my life now had a secret goal—to find the men who had done this horrible thing to my mother. So happy once, now I was like a little sapling which, after a violent storm, puts out only gnarled and twisted branches. . . .

The summers of the following years, for the most part, were spent on our farm in eastern Arkansas where my grandmother lived with a brown hound dog, an old gray riding horse, a temperamental milk cow, and pigs fattening for winter meat. Occasionally we would take a trip to other states, or I would be sent to visit friends or relatives of my parents.

I was in my teens. On one of my visits away from home my mother sent for me. My father had been taken to the hospital. When I arrived home, the doctor told me it was just a matter of time. Daddy was gravely ill. The bottom dropped out of my world.

One night Daddy told Mother to go home and get some sleep. "Daisy will stay with me," he assured her.

When Mother and the nurse had left, I stood looking down at his tired dark face against the white of the bed linen. I saw the wrinkles etched deep by a lifetime of struggle, and I saw a stubborn chin and proud high forehead. I started to cry, softly. He opened his eyes. "Don't cry for me, Daisy," he moaned.

"I know I'm going to die, but—"

I started to protest, but his upraised hand stopped me. He knew I knew, and to deny it would make meaningless the honesty we'd always held to in our lifelong relationship with each other. He said calmly, "I'll be better off." I knew this was so. He had cancer.

"I haven't much to leave you, Daisy, so come close and listen and remember what I have to say to you."

I drew a chair up close and placed my hand in his.

"You're filled with hatred. Hate can destroy you, Daisy. Don't hate white people just because they're white. If you hate, make it count for something. Hate the humiliations we are living under in the South. Hate the discrimination that eats away at the soul of every black man and woman. Hate the insults hurled at us by white scum—and then try to do something about it, or your hate won't spell a thing."

"I'm listening to every word you say, Daddy, and I'll try to do what you say. But rest—you must rest now."

He closed his eyes and shook his head impatiently. "I'll decide when I need rest."

How I loved this strong man who all his life had not been able to use his strength in the way he wanted to. He was forced to suppress it and hold himself back, bow to the white yoke or be cut down. And now that his life was ebbing, he was trying to draw on that reservoir of unused strength to give me a lasting inheritance.

54

"Daisy," he resumed, "nothing's going to change all of a sudden, and any Negro speaking out alone will suffer. But more and more will join him, and the blacks, acting together will one day . . ."

His voice grew faint. I held my breath. Starting afresh, he continued haltingly, "I remember the day of your mother's funeral. I went to the post office for the mail. I had on my best dark suit. When I came out of the post office, there were three young white hoodlums standing on the steps. One of them said, 'Look at that dressed-up ape! You live here, boy?' When I didn't answer, two of them blocked my path and the other one said, 'I know what's wrong, he needs something red on!' He picked up a brush from a paint bucket. It was left there by painters who'd been painting the brick foundation around the buildings. He painted a red streak down the back of my coat. Then they walked away, laughing. I stood there with murder in my heart. I could've crushed the life out of him with my bare hands. But I knew if I touched one hair on his head I could be lynched.

"On my way home I met one of the deputy sheriffs. I showed him my coat and told him what had happened. He laughed and said, 'Don't get so upset about a little thing like that. They were just having a little fun. Turpentine will take the paint out of your coat.' "

Daddy stopped talking and closed his eyes. I just sat there, constantly patting his hard knuckles, hoping he would speak again. He did. This time his voice, still distinct, was softer than before but more labored.

"Sometimes," he said, "you know later when you should have died. I ought to have died the day they put the paint on my coat. I should have taken those guys and wrung their necks like chickens. But I wanted to live—for what, I sometimes wonder."

I stopped patting the back of his hand, and he drifted off into a sleep. Looking at him, I sensed he would never awaken. It was now nearly daybreak. When the Catholic Sister came into the room, I greeted her warmly. It was the first time in several years that I had spoken to a white person in a pleasant voice.

I walked out into the silent streets. The grass, heavy with dew, caught the sun's early rays. In most of the yards flowers still bloomed, and in many, red roses. I thought of another such morning years ago, and of the red rose I couldn't bear to pick. I knew like that rose which clung to its branch in a last, flaming farewell, my father would die before the end of the day. I did not cry now for I realized that he was at peace with himself for the first time in years.

As I walked along the street taking in the freshness of the early morning air, I knew that as surely as my father was dying, I was undergoing a rebirth. My father had passed on to me a priceless heritage—one that was to sustain me throughout the years to come.

Turning Point

Malcolm X

Malcolm X

Malcolm X! The very name cuts through the soul like a well-tempered sword. Malcolm X! In him the warrior in the souls of blacks was made flesh and it is as a warrior that he is now remembered and revered.

He was born in Omaha, Nebraska, in 1925. His father was a Baptist minister and an organizer for the black separatist, Marcus Garvey. When Malcolm was six, his father was murdered by whites because of his militancy. He left eight children, including Malcolm. After some months the state found Malcolm's mother incompetent and declared her insane. She was taken into the State Mental Hospital and the children were sent to foster homes.

Malcolm did not fare well with white foster parents. He spent three years in a detention home and finally, at age sixteen, he was given permission to live with his half-sister, Ella, in Boston. Here, Malcolm began a life of petty crime, eventually going to New York, where in a few years he had become a hustler and dope-pusher. When he was twenty-one he was arrested for armed robbery in Massachusetts and given a ten-year prison sentence.

While in prison, Malcolm began educating himself, taking a correspondence course in English and reading extensively in the prison library. Through his brother, Reginald, he was introduced to the Nation of Islam, sometimes called the Black Muslims. Malcolm studied the teachings of the Honorable Elijah Muhammad, the leader of the Nation of Islam, and became a convert. In accordance with Muslim doctrine, he dropped his last name, Little, and replaced it with X, symbolizing the fact that no American black had his own name, but that of a former slave-owner.

In 1952 he was released and went to Chicago, where Elijah Muhammad gave Malcolm personal instruction. In 1954 he became a Muslim minister. Malcolm became one of the principal organizers for the Nation of Islam, and in the early 1960s he came to national prominence as minister of the Muslim mosque in Harlem.

What Malcolm taught, however, had as great an impact on non-Muslims as it did on Muslims. Malcolm looked upon his role as one of awakening blacks to the realities of their existence. He preached pride in self, black unity, the right of self-defense, and black power. He not only gained converts to the Nation of Islam, but more important, he forged a new black consciousness.

In 1963 Malcolm left the Nation of Islam and founded his own organization, the Muslim Mosque, Inc. He lived scarcely a year after he left the Nation but in that year his thinking continued to grow. He made a pilgrimage to Mecca—the spiritual center of Islam—after which he adopted the Muslim name El Hajj Malik El-Shabazz. He also visited Africa twice—talking to African leaders, enlisting their support for his plan to bring the case of blacks in America before the United Nations, and emphasizing the bonds uniting men of African descent everywhere.

On February 21, 1965, he was assassinated as he started to give his regular Sunday afternoon address at the

Audubon Ballroom in New York City. On that day, however, a mere man was killed. What Malcolm X said and
represented not only did not die that day, but it took on
new life. Today Malcolm X stands as one of the black
saints in history, not only in the United States, but wherever blacks gather in the name of liberation.

———————————

That summer of 1940, in
Lansing, I caught the Greyhound bus for Boston with
my cardboard suitcase, and wearing my green suit.
If someone had hung a sign, "HICK," around my
neck, I couldn't have looked much more obvious.
They didn't have the turnpikes then; the bus stopped
at what seemed every corner and cowpatch. From my
seat in—you guessed it—the back of the bus, I
gawked out of the window at white man's America
rolling past for what seemed a month, but must have
been only a day and a half.

When we finally arrived, Ella met me at the ter-
minal and took me home. The house was on Waum-
beck Street in the Sugar Hill section of Roxbury, the
Harlem of Boston. I met Ella's second husband, Frank,
who was now a soldier; and her brother Earl, the
singer who called himself Jimmy Carleton; and Mary,
who was very different from her older sister. It's funny

how I seemed to think of Mary as Ella's sister, instead of her being, just as Ella is, my own half-sister. It's probably because Ella and I always were much closer as basic types; we're dominant people, and Mary has always been mild and quiet, almost shy.

Ella was busily involved in dozens of things. She belonged to I don't know how many different clubs; she was a leading light of local so-called "black society." I saw and met a hundred black people there whose big-city talk and ways left my mouth hanging open.

I couldn't have feigned indifference if I had tried to. People talked casually about Chicago, Detroit, New York. I didn't know the world contained as many Negroes as I saw thronging downtown Roxbury at night, especially on Saturdays. Neon lights, nightclubs, poolhalls, bars, the cars they drove! Restaurants made the streets smell—rich, greasy, down-home black cooking! Juke-boxes blared Erskine Hawkins, Duke Ellington, Cootie Williams, dozens of others. If somebody had told me then that some day I'd know them all personally, I'd have found it hard to believe. The biggest bands, like these, played at the Roseland State Ballroom, on Boston's Massachusetts Avenue—one night for Negroes, the next night for whites.

I saw for the first time occasional white-black couples strolling around arm in arm. And on Sundays, when Ella, Mary, or somebody took me to church, I

62

saw churches for black people such as I had never seen. They were many times finer than the white church I had attended back in Mason, Michigan. There, the white people just sat and worshiped with words; but the Boston Negroes, like all other Negroes I had ever seen at church, threw their souls and bodies wholly into worship.

Two or three times, I wrote letters to Wilfred [my oldest brother] intended for everybody back in Lansing. I said I'd try to describe it when I got back.

But I found I couldn't.

My restlessness with Mason—and for the first time in my life a restlessness with being around white people—began as soon as I got back home and entered eighth grade.

I continued to think constantly about all that I had seen in Boston, and about the way I had felt there. I know now that it was the sense of being a real part of a mass of my own kind, for the first time.

The white people—classmates, the Swerlins, the people at the restaurant where I worked—noticed the change. They said, "You're acting so strange. You don't seem like yourself, Malcolm. What's the matter?"

I kept close to the top of the class, though. The topmost scholastic standing, I remember, kept shifting between me, a girl named Audrey Slaugh, and a boy named Jimmy Cotton.

It went on that way, as I became increasingly restless and disturbed through the first semester. And then one day, just about when those of us who had passed were about to move up to 8-A, from which we would enter high school the next year, something happened which was to become the first major turning point of my life.

Somehow, I happened to be alone in the classroom with Mr. Ostrowski, my English teacher. He was a tall, rather reddish white man and he had a thick mustache. I had gotten some of my best marks under him, and he had always made me feel that he liked me. He was a natural-born "advisor," about what you ought to read, to do, or think—about any and everything. We used to make unkind jokes about him: why was he teaching in Mason instead of somewhere else, getting for himself some of the "success in life" that he kept telling us how to get?

I know that he probably meant well in what he happened to advise me that day. I doubt that he meant any harm. It was just in his nature as an American white man. I was one of his top students, one of the school's top students—but all he could see for me was the kind of future "in your place" that almost all white people see for black people.

He told me, "Malcolm, you ought to be thinking about a career. Have you been giving it thought?"

The truth is, I hadn't. I never have figured out why I told him, "Well, yes, sir, I've been thinking I'd like to be a lawyer." Lansing certainly had no Negro lawyers—or doctors either—in those days, to hold up an image I might have aspired to. All I really knew for certain was that a lawyer didn't wash dishes, as I was doing.

Mr. Ostrowski looked surprised, I remember, and leaned back in his chair and clasped his hands behind his head. He kind of half-smiled and said, "Malcolm, one of life's first needs is for us to be realistic. Don't misunderstand me, now. We all here like you, you know that. But you've got to be realistic about being a nigger. A lawyer—that's no realistic goal for a nigger. You need to think about something you *can* be. You're good with your hands—making things. Everybody admires your carpentry shop work. Why don't you plan on carpentry? People like you as a person—you'd get all kinds of work."

The more I thought afterwards about what he said, the more uneasy it made me. It just kept treading around in my mind.

What made it really begin to disturb me was Mr. Ostrowski's advice to others in my class—all of them white. Most of them had told him they were planning to become farmers, like their parents—to one day take over their family farms. But those who wanted to strike out on their own, to try something new, he had encouraged. Some, mostly girls, wanted to be teachers. A few wanted other professions, such as one boy who wanted to become a county agent; another, a veterinarian; and one girl wanted to be a nurse. They all reported that Mr. Ostrowski had encouraged whatever they had wanted. Yet nearly none of them had earned marks equal to mine.

It was a surprising thing that I had never thought of it that way before, but I realized that whatever I wasn't, I *was* smarter than nearly all of those white kids. But apparently I was still not intelligent enough, in their eyes, to become whatever *I* wanted to be.

It was then that I began to change—inside.

I drew away from white people. I came to class, and I answered when called upon. It became a physical strain simply to sit in Mr. Ostrowski's class.

Where "nigger" had slipped off my back before, wherever I heard it now, I stopped and looked at whoever said it. And they looked surprised that I did.

I quit hearing so much "nigger" and "What's wrong?"—which was the way I wanted it. Nobody, including the teachers, could decide what had come over me. I knew I was being discussed.

In a few more weeks, it was that way, too, at the restaurant where I worked washing dishes, and at the Swerlins'.

One day soon after, Mrs. Swerlin called me into the living room, and there was the state man, Maynard Allen. I knew from their faces that something was about to happen. She told me that none of them could understand why—after I had done so well in school, and on my job, and living with them, and after everyone in Mason had come to like me—I had lately begun to make them all feel that I wasn't happy there anymore.

She said she felt there was no need for me to stay at the detention home any longer, and that arrangements had been made for me to go and live with the Lyons family, who liked me so much.

She stood up and put out her hand. "I guess I've asked you a hundred times, Malcolm—do you want to tell me what's wrong?"

I shook her hand, and said, "Nothing, Mrs. Swerlin." Then I went to get my things, and came back down. At the living room door I saw her wiping her eyes. I felt very bad. I thanked her and went out in front to Mr. Allen, who took me over to the Lyons'.

Mr. and Mrs. Lyons, and their children, during the two months I lived with them—while finishing eighth grade—also tried to get me to tell them what was wrong. But somehow I couldn't tell them, either.

I went every Saturday to see my brothers and sisters in Lansing, and almost every other day I wrote to Ella in Boston. Not saying why, I told Ella that I wanted to come there and live.

I don't know how she did it, but she arranged for official custody of me to be transferred from Michigan to Massachusetts, and the very week I finished the eighth grade, I again boarded the Greyhound bus for Boston.

I've thought about that time a lot since then. No physical move in my life has been more pivotal or profound in its repercussions.

If I had stayed on in Michigan, I would probably have married one of those Negro girls I knew and liked in Lansing. I might have become one of those state capitol building shoeshine boys, or a Lansing Country Club waiter, or gotten one of the other menial jobs which, in those days, among Lansing Negroes, would have been considered "successful"—or even become a carpenter.

Whatever I have done since then, I have driven myself to become a success at it. I've often thought that if Mr. Ostrowski had encouraged me to become a lawyer, I would today probably be among some city's professional black bourgeoisie, sipping cocktails and palming myself off as a community spokesman for and leader of the suffering black masses, while my primary concern would be to grab a few more crumbs from the groaning board of the two-faced whites with whom they're begging to "integrate."

All praise is due to Allah that I went to Boston when I did. If I hadn't, I'd probably still be a brainwashed black Christian.

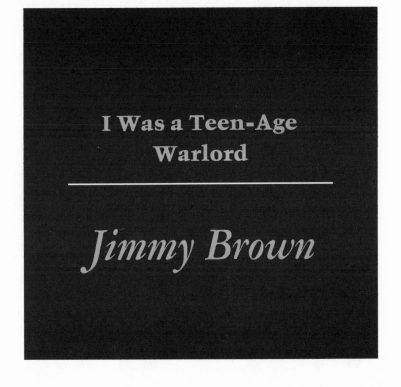

I Was a Teen-Age
Warlord

Jimmy Brown

Jimmy Brown

In the annals of professional football, the name of Jimmy Brown holds a special place. He played nine years with the Cleveland Browns. In that time he came to be regarded by many as the greatest fullback ever to put on a pair of cleated shoes and step onto the football field. He still holds the career record for the most yards gained rushing. And in 1963 he established a National Football League one-season record of 1,863 yards gained, which has yet to be broken.

He was born on St. Simons Island, Georgia, and spent the first eight years of his life there. He was raised by his great-grandmother, his mother having gone to New York to work shortly after separating from his father while Jim was still an infant.

When he was nine his mother sent for him and he moved north to Long Island, where his mother worked as a domestic. Jim attended school in Manhasset. While in high school he began to develop his native athletic ability. Even as a child, Jim had been very strong and muscular—so much so that the children of St. Simons had nicknamed him "Man." His high school football career was so brilliant that he had offers from forty-five colleges.

Eventually he decided to attend Syracuse University, where he starred not only in football, but also in track, lacrosse, and basketball. Upon graduation, he was drafted by the Cleveland Browns and quickly established himself as a star in his rookie year. He became the most feared runner in the game and one of the most exciting to watch.

Once he had established himself, however, Brown shocked the staid athletic world by showing himself to be a man to fear off the field as well as on. He began to speak his mind about discrimination and racism within professional football and elsewhere in America. One of the myths of athletics is that it is an example of successful integration. As long as black athletes kept silent, it was. Jim Brown could not keep silent. With the publication of his autobiography, *Off My Chest*, in 1964 he created a good deal of controversy with what were then radical views on race.

In 1966 he retired from professional football to begin what has become a very successful career as a movie actor. Together with other well-known athletes, he also started an organization—the Black Economic Union (formerly the Negro Industrial and Economic Union). This organization gives loans to blacks wanting to start in business and also acts as a consultant to established black businesses.

On the field and off, Jimmy Brown has—for some years now—been a symbol of black manhood and aggressiveness. He has not allowed his fame or his wealth to separate him from the masses of blacks.

In the selection below from *Off My Chest*, Brown relates the story of his life in the North as a gang leader and high school football star.

———————◆———————

When I first arrived in the North at the age of nine, my mother was employed by a Jewish family—the Brockmans—who lived in the well-to-do, all-white suburb of Great Neck, Long Island. They provided us with a small one-bedroom apartment off the kitchen. However, I had to attend school several miles away in Manhasset, a community that ranged from comfortably middle class to very poor. The poor lived in an area called "the Valley," which was ripe with slums that made the community fathers wince. Visible to motorists passing down Northern Boulevard through Manhasset, the slums were regarded as a bad advertisement for the town and later were torn down and replaced by a park and a housing project.

In Manhasset, Nate Brown became Jimmy Brown. At school I enrolled as James Nathaniel Brown, so the teachers called me James and the kids made it Jimmy. Many of the kids in my elementary school were from the poor Valley district, and I found out my first day in school that the student body was tough. I wasted no time fighting my way to the top.

That first day, my mother dressed me neat-as-a-pin in a starched shirt and creased trousers; she brushed my hair and sent me off to school in a taxi. The student body took note of my arrival. At recess in the schoolyard, a Negro boy—no bigger nor smaller than I—addressed me. "You look real pretty, Sis," he said, and promptly shoved me back on my heels. "Well, good," I thought. Manhasset was going to be just as playful as St. Simons Island. I knocked him down and dove on top of him and began punching the daylights out of him. "Dirty fighter!" all the kids hollered. I stopped punching and looked up, mystified. Down on the island, this was the way we always fought. The purpose of knocking someone down was to sit on him and get in the best licks. Nobody back home called it dirty fighting.

Anyhow, while I was trying to decide whether to go on, a man whom the kids called Bulldog Drummond strode into the schoolyard and yanked me off my new friend. Bulldog Drummond was the school principal, Mr. Hutchens. The kids had named him after the hero of the radio program because Mr. Hutchens had a square jaw and was old-fashioned tough.

"I'll show you how we settle these things here," Mr. Hutchens told me. He marched us into the gym and handed us boxing gloves. I'd never seen a pair of boxing gloves. My opponent, having been marched to the gym by Mr. Hutchens on previous occasions, knew how to use the gloves. He gave me a licking. "These northerners have a funny way of doing things," I thought, but out of sight of Mr. Hutchens I managed to win all my fights and become known as a tough guy. My mother continued to send me off to school in a taxi, all starched and spotless.

The Brockmans were wonderful people to live with. They bought me my first basketball and hung a basket for me in the yard. They did more things for me than I can remember, and even after they moved to Los Angeles several years later, they continued to correspond with my mother and send her gifts. I would have liked to have lived with the Brockmans all my boyhood, but after perhaps two years there I was too old to live with my mother in a one-bedroom apartment. The Brockmans, with children of their own, had given us all the space they could, so my mother roomed me out with a Negro family in Manhasset.

I wasn't happy in Manhasset. The lady of the house was very religious. She was, no doubt, a good woman but quite stern. Somehow, I felt like an intruder.

Happily, I always saw my mother on weekends. I loved my mother as much as any son would, and yet I was never able to bring myself to call her mama. Mama was my great-grandmother, down on St. Si-

75

mons. I didn't know what to call my mother. Once in a while I called her mother, but the word always sounded strange on my lips. I had known affection from my great-grandmother and had returned it, but was never able to demonstrate, overtly, my affection for my mother. This hurt her, I know. But in a way, I had two mothers, and mama had gotten there first.

When the Brockmans moved to Los Angeles, my mother took a first-floor flat in Manhasset and brought me to live with her again, and I was happy once more. Her expenses were higher and she had trouble finding enough work, but with a lot of scraping she managed to keep me neatly dressed. My neatness had become a point of pride with me, and later, my high school football coach, Ed Walsh, came to realize this. "How'd you like to take a trip into Manhattan with me tomorrow?" he said to me one day. The next day I found myself standing in a Howard's store, where Ed Walsh had me fitted for a fine suit.

My coaches and teachers were the big people in my life. The Lord knows, they had their work cut out for them in trying to make something of me, but they went at it.

I had no interest in studies and, what's more, had become president and official warlord of a teen-age gang known as the Gaylords. We held dances and parties and with the ticket receipts decked ourselves out in reversible jackets—base black with orchid trim on one side and base orchid with black trim on the other. We had our gang name lettered across our backs and our own names in front. The jackets were a big deal.

Many teen-age gangs roamed a string of communities across Long Island, picking up girls and attending rival gangs' parties uninvited. Our Long Island gangs, however, were not of the zip gun variety known to Brooklyn. Our boys carried switchblade penknives but only to build up their own egos. They liked to stand on street corners clicking their knives, but they never used them in fights. Fights generally wound up with an enactment of the *West Side Story* bit—that is, warlord pitted against warlord, with everyone else forming a circle.

As warlord of the Gaylords, I rarely had to fight, simply because my opponents almost always backed down. Since my first year on Long Island—the year I'd fought my way to the top of the class—I'd had a fairly formidable reputation. Still, I should have known that sooner or later I'd have to face a blade. One night in Hempstead I did.

We had invited ourselves to a party being held by a rival gang. For a while, all was peaceful. I was just standing there, listening to the phonograph music and minding my own business. The rival warlord, however, had been drinking liquor and growing belligerent on it. He swayed with the music and snapped his fingers and then, pretending to be only releasing his feeling for the music, gave me a hard slap on the back. I knew he meant it as a challenge. I said nothing. He slapped me a second time, and I told him, "Look, don't slap me on the back." I moved a few steps away. "Oh, you think you're something big?" he said. "You guys come in here in your sharp jackets and think you're something." I said to myself, "Here it goes." I told him, "Look, we can settle this fast. Just come outside." He got loud. "Sure I'll come outside," he shouted for everyone to hear. "I'll wipe up the street with you." We went outside, and everyone crowded around us. Then, click! Out came his blade.

I had no knife myself. I never carried one, because I never believed a knife would make me any bigger and I knew I could never cut anyone. Now I had to think fast. I reached into my pocket and held my hand there for a menacing moment. All I had in it was a ringful of keys. With a great show of purpose, I worked one key into position so that it pointed sharply against my trousers. Then I whipped my hand from my pocket. The instant I did, my opponent closed his knife and shoved it into his pocket. He smiled weakly. I opened the palm of my hand, revealing a fistful of keys, and then hauled off with my other hand—also open—and gave him a hard slap in the face. End of *West Side Story* bit. "Let's go home," I said to the Gaylords.

Actually, I guess I never quite fit the image of a

gang warlord. Though I never minded a fight, I never picked one and I disliked bullies. Kids sometimes teased me for not smoking or drinking liquor, but I couldn't see how a cigaret dangling from the corner of my mouth could make me any tougher. Then, too, I was coming to realize that my physical strength could be put to better use on a ball field than in fist fights.

A succession of great men—men who were great simply because they cared—had come into my life:

First, there was Jay Stranahan, coach of the basketball, lacrosse, and six-man football teams at Plandome Road Junior High. "Jimmy, you have tremendous athletic ability," he told me. "Don't waste it." There had been no such thing as football on St. Simons Island; the first game I'd seen in Manhasset had been on a corner lot that had been picked clean of rocks and broken glass. Now Jay Stranahan was telling me that I could play this game—and lacrosse and basketball, too—better than any kid in school, and he meant to give me no time to get into trouble.

Then there was Jack Peploe, a cop. Patrolman Jack Peploe, today superintendent of parks and grounds for Nassau County, ran the Police Boys Club. He put me in charge of the Boys Club basketball team. He gave me the keys to the high school gym and appointed me the big shot to open the gym every night.

There were others—people all around me who without hesitation went out of their way to make something of me. Mrs. Virginia Hansen, a speech teacher, observed that I was a quiet kid. She forced me to make two- and three-minute speeches in school and brought me to the point where I became a self-assured assembly speaker. Al Dawson, the high school track coach, worked tirelessly to develop my skills. Dr. Raymond L. Collins, superintendent of Manhasset schools, took me to the school gym Sunday afternoons to shoot baskets with him and his son. (Dr. Collins was an old-fashioned underhand set shooter but probably the deadliest shot of all school superintendents in the country.) In short, what I received from these adults around me was love. I was a poor kid from a broken home but I was not insecure, because where there is love there cannot be insecurity. Even when I was a little guy on St. Simons Island, mama and I never felt insecure because we loved one another and knew that come what may, we were not alone.

At Manhasset High School there was a football coach named Ed Walsh, and I will tell you about him because he was my idea of a saint. He was a slender, soft-spoken man but one whose actions made you realize that real strength was not physical strength but strength of character. I am convinced that Ed Walsh had not one iota of bigotry in him. Moreover, of all the football coaches I've played for, Ed, a mere high school coach, was the finest—the most expert.

Even today, when I find it necessary to refresh my knowledge of fundamentals, I say to myself, "Let's see, how did Ed Walsh teach that move?" In the four years I played for him, his teams lost only two games —one by a touchdown and the other by a single point. Because he had movies made of his games, I've been able to go back to Manhasset from time to time and watch myself in action as a high school halfback. It's hard to believe, but I made better moves and cuts in high school than I've made in college and pro ball, and that's a fact.

More than a great teacher of football technique, Ed Walsh was a builder of character. He cared about his kids, and would reach into his own pocket to buy a needy student clothing. I had a childish spat with my mother once and told Ed I was going to leave home. "Come out and stay at my house a while," he told me, "until you've had a chance to think it over and you're sure you're doing the right thing." It was no phony gesture but a sincere invitation.

"You can be a professional football player," he told me on another occasion. "But you've got to go to college first, and you won't go to college unless you start taking your studies seriously." I began taking my studies seriously. In time I was nominated for student body president but said I wouldn't run, because I knew that if I were elected it would be only because of my popularity as an athlete. I felt one of the topmost students should be president. So I was elected chief justice of the student court, which though a lesser post was a step up from gang warlord.

"Okay, Jimmy," Ed Walsh barked at me one day in football scrimmage. "If you want to loaf get off the first team. Get over there on defense with the second team." I went over to the defense and did all I could to tear the first team apart. The next day I was back on the first team. The point is, I had to get back into Ed Walsh's good graces at all costs, not so much because I disliked being second-string but because I had let him down. Since that day I've never messed up on a coach of his stripe—that is, a coach I could talk to and reason with and who would give me the benefit of the doubt in a tough spot.

Sitting In and
Hiding Out

Anne Moody

Anne Moody

Among the most courageous youth that America has ever seen are those young men and women who worked in the South as civil rights workers during the 1960s. The task which they set themselves was to organize the poor blacks of the South to fight for the right to be treated as citizens under the law.

It sounded simple, but it wasn't. The white South was organized to see that blacks did not get those rights. The blacks of the South, having lived in fear for generations, were not easily organized to demonstrate or protest against their subjugation. Blacks had been murdered for refusing to step off the sidewalk when a white person was coming toward them. The young civil rights worker had first to overcome the very real fears of the black community, as well as resist the attempts of whites to scare them away.

One of these civil rights workers was Anne Moody. Unlike some of the workers who came to the South from the North, she was born and raised on a plantation in Wilkinson County, Mississippi. Anne herself knew the fear—it had been taught to her from childhood. She knew the slavery of plantation life and what it meant to be a sharecropper as her parents were. She knew what it was to be hungry and cold. When she was nine years old, Anne worked as a maid for white people because the little she could earn was needed to help support her brothers and sisters. She knew and yet she refused to succumb to total despair.

When she became a teen-ager, Anne began spending her summers in Baton Rouge or New Orleans, Louisiana, working. It was menial work, but at least she wasn't working in the cotton fields. And being in the cities broadened her consciousness, raised her aspirations, and made her dissatisfied with life on a Mississippi plantation. She finished high school in Wilkinson County and attended Natchez Junior College and, in 1964, graduated from Tougaloo College in Tougaloo, Mississippi.

By the time of her college graduation, however, Anne was a veteran of the civil rights movement. She had participated in sit-ins at dime store lunch counters and had become acquainted with many of the civil rights workers from the Student Non-Violent Coordinating Committee and the Congress of Racial Equality. Most of them had been arrested repeatedly, beaten, and some even wounded or killed. Anne was not afraid to take the same risks and—in 1963—she went to Canton, Mississippi, to help organize the local blacks to register as voters.

Canton is a small town near Jackson, the capital, with a reputation designed to instill fear into the heart of any black person. It is one of those towns where if the sheriff says "Nigger, be out of town by sundown," the listener knows that he is not hearing bad dialogue from a bad movie. It was here that Anne Moody and other CORE workers went to organize and it was here that her own life was put in mortal danger.

The selection below is from her autobiography, *Coming of Age in Mississippi.*

———————◆———————

Things didn't seem to be coming along too well in the Delta. On Saturdays we would spend all day canvassing and often at night we would have mass rallies. But these were usually poorly attended. Many Negroes were afraid to come. In the beginning some were even afraid to talk to us. Most of these old plantation Negroes had been brainwashed so by the whites, they really thought that only whites were supposed to vote. There were even a few who had never heard of voting. The only thing most of them knew was how to handle a hoe. For years they had demonstrated how well they could do that. Some of them had calluses on their hands so thick they would hide them if they noticed you looking at them.

On Sundays we usually went to Negro churches to speak. We were split into groups according to our religious affiliation. We were supposed to know how to reach those with the same faith as ourselves. In church we hoped to be able to reach many more Negroes. We knew that even those that slammed doors in our faces or said, "I don't want no part of voting" would be there. There would also be the schoolteachers and the middle-class professional Negroes who dared not participate. They knew that once they did, they would lose that $250 a month job. But the people started getting wise to us. Most of them stopped coming to church. They knew if they came, they would have to face us. Then the ministers started asking us not to come because we scared their congregations away. SNCC had to come up with a new strategy.

As the work continued that summer, people began to come around. I guess they saw that our intentions were good. But some began getting fired from their jobs, thrown off plantations and left homeless. They could often find somewhere else to stay, but food and clothing became a problem. SNCC started to send representatives to Northern college campuses. They went begging for food, clothing and money for the people in Mississippi, and the food, clothing and money started coming in. The Delta Negroes still didn't understand the voting, but they knew they had found friends, friends they could trust.

That summer I could feel myself beginning to change. For the first time I began to think something would be done about whites killing, beating, and misusing Negroes. I knew I was going to be a part of whatever happened. . . .

I had counted on graduating in the spring of 1963,

but as it turned out, I couldn't because some of my credits still had to be cleared with Natchez College. A year before, this would have seemed like a terrible disaster, but now I hardly even felt disappointed. I had a good excuse to stay on campus for the summer and work with the Movement, and this was what I really wanted to do. I couldn't go home again anyway, and I couldn't go to New Orleans [where my aunt lived]—I didn't have money enough for bus fare.

During my senior year at Tougaloo, my family hadn't sent me one penny. I had only the small amount of money I had earned at Maple Hill. I couldn't afford to eat at school or live in the dorms, so I had gotten permission to move off campus.

I had to prove that I could finish school, even if I had to go hungry every day. I knew Raymond and Miss Pearl [my step-father and his mother] were just waiting to see me drop out. But something happened to me as I got more and more involved in the Movement. It no longer seemed important to prove anything. I had found something outside myself that gave meaning to my life.

I had become very friendly with my social science professor, John Salter, who was in charge of NAACP activities on campus. All during the year, while the NAACP conducted a boycott of the downtown stores in Jackson, I had been one of Salter's most faithful canvassers and church speakers. During the last week of school, he told me that sit-in demonstrations were about to start in Jackson and that he wanted me to be the spokesman for a team that would sit-in at Woolworth's lunch counter.

The two other demonstrators would be classmates of mine, Memphis and Pearlena. Pearlena was a dedicated NAACP worker, but Memphis had not been very involved in the Movement on campus. It seemed that the organization had had a rough time finding students who were in a position to go to jail. I had nothing to lose one way or the other.

Around ten o'clock the morning of the demonstrations, NAACP headquarters alerted the news services. As a result, the police department was also informed, but neither the policemen nor the newsmen knew exactly where or when the demonstrations would start. They stationed themselves along Capitol Street and waited.

To divert attention from the sit-in at Woolworth's, the picketing started at J. C. Penney's a good fifteen minutes before. The pickets were allowed to walk up and down in front of the store three or four times before they were arrested.

At exactly 11 A.M., Pearlena, Memphis, and I entered Woolworth's from the rear entrance. We separated as soon as we stepped into the store, and made small purchases from various counters. Pearlena had given Memphis her watch. He was to let us know when it was 11:14. At 11:14 we were to join him near the lunch counter and at exactly 11:15 we were to take seats at it.

Seconds before 11:15 we were occupying three seats at the previously segregated Woolworth's lunch counter. In the beginning the waitresses seemed to ignore us, as if they really didn't know what was going on.

Our waitress walked past us a couple of times before she noticed we had started to write our orders down and realized we wanted service. She asked us what we wanted.

We began to read to her from our order slips.

She told us that we would be served at the back counter, which was for Negroes.

"We would like to be served here," I said.

The waitress started to repeat what she had said, then stopped in the middle of the sentence. She turned the lights out behind the counter, and she and the other waitresses almost ran to the back of the store, deserting all their white customers. I guess they thought that violence would start immediately after the whites at the counter realized what was going on.

There were five or six other people at the counter. A couple of them just got up and walked away. A girl sitting next to me finished her banana split before leaving. A middle-aged white woman who had not yet been served rose from her seat and came over to us.

"I'd like to stay here with you," she said, "but my husband is waiting."

The newsmen came in just as she was leaving. They must have discovered what was going on shortly after some of the people began to leave the store.

One of the newsmen ran behind the woman who spoke to us and asked her to identify herself. She refused to give her name, but said she was a native of Vicksburg and a former resident of California. When asked why she had said what she had said to us, she replied, "I am in sympathy with the Negro movement."

By this time a crowd of cameramen and reporters had gathered around us taking pictures and asking questions, such as Where were we from? Why did we sit-in? What organization sponsored it? Were we students? From what school? How were we classified?

I told them that we were all students at Tougaloo College, that we were represented by no particular organization, and that we planned to stay there even after the store closed. "All we want is service," was my reply to one of them. After they had finished probing for about twenty minutes, they were almost ready to leave.

At noon, students from a nearby white high school started pouring in to Woolworth's. When they first saw us they were sort of surprised. They didn't know how to react. A few started to heckle and the newsmen became interested again. Then the white students started chanting all kinds of anti-Negro slogans. We were called a little bit of everything.

The rest of the seats except the three we were occupying had been roped off to prevent others from sitting down. A couple of the boys took one end of the rope and made it into a hangman's noose. Several attempts were made to put it around our necks. The crowds grew as more students and adults came in for lunch.

We kept our eyes straight forward and did not look at the crowd except for occasional glances to see what was going on. All of a sudden I saw a face I remembered—the drunkard from the bus station sit-in. My eyes lingered on him just long enough for us to recognize each other. Today he was drunk too, so I don't think he remembered where he had seen me before. He took out a knife, opened it, put it in his pocket, and then began to pace the floor.

At this point, I told Memphis and Pearlena what was going on. Memphis suggested that we pray. We bowed our heads, and all hell broke loose. A man rushed forward, threw Memphis from his seat, and slapped my face. Then another man who worked in the store threw me against an adjoining counter.

Down on my knees on the floor, I saw Memphis lying near the lunch counter with blood running out of the corners of his mouth. As he tried to protect his face, the man who'd thrown him down kept kicking him against the head. If he had worn hard-soled shoes instead of sneakers, the first kick probably would have killed Memphis. Finally a man dressed in plain clothes identified himself as a police officer and arrested Memphis and his attacker.

Pearlena had been thrown to the floor. She and I got back on our stools after Memphis was arrested. There were some white Tougaloo teachers in the crowd. They asked Pearlena and me if we wanted to leave. They said that things were getting too rough. We didn't know what to do. While we were trying to make up our minds, we were joined by Joan Trumpauer. Now there were three of us and we were integrated.

The crowd began to chant, "Communists, Communists, Communists." Some old man in the crowd ordered the students to take us off the stools.

"Which one should I get first?" a big husky boy said.

"That white nigger," the old man said.

The boy lifted Joan from the counter by her waist and carried her out of the store. Simultaneously, I was snatched from my stool by two high school students. I was dragged about thirty feet toward the door by my hair when someone made them turn me loose. As I was getting up off the floor, I saw Joan coming back inside. We started back to the center of the counter to join Pearlena. Lois Chaffee, a white Tougaloo faculty member, was now sitting next to her. So Joan and I just climbed across the rope at the front end of the counter and sat down. There were now four of us, two whites and two Negroes, all women.

The mob started smearing us with ketchup, mustard, sugar, pies, and everything on the counter. Soon Joan and I were joined by John Salter, but the moment he sat down he was hit on the jaw with what appeared to be brass knuckles. Blood gushed from his face and someone threw salt into the open wound. Ed King, Tougaloo's chaplain, rushed to him.

At the other end of the counter, Lois and Pearlena were joined by George Raymond, a CORE field worker and a student from Jackson State College. Then a Negro high school boy sat down next to me. The mob took spray paint from the counter and sprayed it on the new demonstrators. The high school student had on a white shirt; the word "nigger" was written on his back with red spray paint.

We sat there for three hours taking a beating when the manager decided to close the store because the mob had begun to go wild with stuff from other counters. He begged and begged everyone to leave. But even after fifteen minutes of begging, no one budged. They would not leave until we did. Then Dr. Beittel, the president of Tougaloo College, came running in. He said he had just heard what was happening.

95

About ninety policemen were standing outside the store; they had been watching the whole thing through the windows, but had not come in to stop the mob or do anything. President Beittel went outside and asked Captain Ray to come and escort us out. The captain refused, stating the manager had to invite him in before he could enter the premises, so Dr. Beittel himself brought us out. He had told the police that they had better protect us after we were outside the store.

When we got outside, the policemen formed a single line that blocked the mob from us. However, they were allowed to throw at us everything they had collected. Within ten minutes, we were picked up by Reverend King in his station wagon and taken to the NAACP headquarters on Lynch Street.

After the sit-in, all I could think of was how sick Mississippi whites were. They believed so much in the segregated Southern way of life, they would kill to preserve it. I sat there in the NAACP office and thought of how many times they had killed when this way of life was threatened. I knew that the killing had just begun. "Many more will die before it is over with," I thought.

Before the sit-in, I had always hated the whites in Mississippi. Now I knew it was impossible for me to hate sickness. The whites had a disease, an incurable disease in its final stage. What were our chances against such a disease? I thought of the students, the young Negroes who had just begun to protest, as young interns. When these young interns got older, I thought, they would be the best doctors in the world for social problems. . . .

[That summer Anne went to work with CORE in Canton. Their strongest local support came from C. O. Chinn and his wife, a well-established black family. With the other workers, Anne lived in the newly built Freedom House, which had been provided by Mrs. Chinn's brother, Sonny.]

One Friday evening, just as we were finishing dinner, Sonny's brother Robert came running into the kitchen. He was sweating and panting as if he had been running for a long time. At first, he didn't say anything. We all sat and stared, waiting. He just stared back. He looked like he was trying to decide how to tell us something. I thought that he had been chased by someone.

"Man, what's wrong with you?" George finally asked.

"Uh . . . uh . . ." Robert began. "Man, y'all better get outta Canton *tonight!* I got a funny feelin' when I was walkin' aroun' in town tonight so I went over to that Black Tom's café to see what people were talkin' 'bout. Sho' nuff, one o' them drunk bastards sittin' up there sayin' they gonna kill all them damn freedom workers tonight."

"What? *Who* said that?" Jerome Smith yelled. "You

97

got more sense, Robert, than to go believe what you hear some drunkard sayin' in a café."

"Man, lissen, lissen, you don't believe me, go ask Joe Lee. He was sittin' there a *long* time. He said he was just about to come over and tell y'all. They really gonna do it, they really gonna do it tonight! Did Dave go to Jackson yet? Man, y'all better get outta Canton!"

"What do you mean, Robert?" I asked. "How did that guy find out? Them whites probably spread that shit just so it'll get back to us. If they were really gonna kill us, wouldn't any nigger in town know anything about it till it was all over with."

"Moody, that man work for Howard, who's behind *all* this shit here in Canton, and if he say he heard somethin', he *heard* it."

"That's what I just said, it was intended for him to hear," I said.

"George, y'all can sit here and listen to Annie Moody if you want to, but I swear to *God*, you betta get outta here! You think that fuckin nigger woulda said anything if he *hadn'ta* been drunk?"

It was hard for us to believe what Robert was saying; however, none of us had ever seen him this nervous before. Finally George and Jerome decided that they would go into town to see if they could find out anything. By the time they got back it was pitch black outside. As soon as Jerome burst in the door we could all see that Robert had been right.

"Them white folks in town's *together*, man, and we better do something but quick," he said, almost out of breath.

I knew we were in bad shape. Dave had taken the car into Jackson for the weekend and the only people in town that would put us up were C.O. and Minnie Lou and they weren't home. So we just sat there until after eleven, trying to figure out a way to get out of Canton. We couldn't walk because there was only one way in and one way out, and we knew they could just as well mow us down on the highway.

"We are just wastin' time sittin' here bullshittin' like this. I ain't about to go down that dark-ass road. And I ain't about to stay in this damn house either," Flukie said.

"Y'all can sit here and talk *all night* if you want to," Bettye said, suddenly appearing in the door with a blanket in her arms. "But I'm gonna take my ass out back in that tall grass and worry about gettin' outta here tomorrow."

Since Sonny's house was new, he hadn't cultivated a garden yet, so the space behind the house where the garden would have been had grown wild with tall weeds. Sonny them just mowed the back lawn right up to the weeds and let them grow like hedges.

It didn't take us long to agree that the weeds were our only way out. Even so, we knew that there was still a good chance that we would be discovered back there, but we had no other choice. So we pulled open the curtains and left the lamps on dim so that anyone could see that the house was empty. We also removed the sheets and blankets and left the spreads so the beds looked made. We waited until about twelve-thirty when all the lights in the neighborhood had been turned out. Then we sneaked out back with blankets and sheets clutched in our arms. The nine of us spaced ourselves so that from a distance no one patch of grass would look mashed down. The five guys made us girls stay behind them. We agreed not to do anything but look and listen without saying a word to each other.

I was wrapped in one of the spreads and after lying still for what seemed like hours, I began to get very cold and stiff. I couldn't hear a sound not even a cricket and I began to feel like I was all alone out there. I listened for Bettye's breathing, but I heard nothing. I wondered if the others were feeling as alone and scared as I was. I could feel the grass getting wet with dew and I began to get colder and colder. I kept thinking about what might happen to us if they found us out there. I tried hard not to think about it. But I couldn't help it. I could see them stomping us in the face and shooting us. I also kept thinking about the house and whether we had left some clue that we were out back. Suddenly I heard a noise and I could almost feel everyone jump with me.

"Don't get scared, it's that damn dog next door. Just be quiet and he'll shut up," one of the guys whispered.

Now I knew we were in for it. That damn dog kept on whimpering. I could see the neighbor coming out and discovering us just when the Klan drove up. But finally the dog was quiet again.

I must have begun to doze off when I heard a car door slam.

"Quiet! Quiet! They're here," Flukie whispered as someone moved in the grass.

I couldn't even breathe. My whole chest began to hurt as I heard the mumbling voices toward the front of the house. When the mumbling got louder I knew that they were in the back. But I still couldn't make out what they were saying. As I heard them moving around in the backyard, I had a horrible feeling that they could see us as plain as daylight and I just trembled all over. But in a few minutes I heard the car door slam again and they were gone.

We lay quietly in case they had pulled a trick. Finally Jerome whispered loudly, "They think we're at C.O.'s. They'll probably be back."

Soon the roosters were crowing and it began to get light. Sure enough they drove up again but this time they must have just taken a quick look, because they were gone almost immediately. We knew they wouldn't be back because it was too light. So we sneaked back in the house before the neighbors got up.

George, who had been in a position to see and hear them, told us what happened. He said that there was a pickup truck with about eight men who had obviously been drinking. They had all sorts of weapons. They discussed burning the house down, but decided that they would come back and get us another night.

After this incident, Robert and a group of men all in their middle or late twenties formed a group to protect us. Three or four of them had already lost their jobs because they tried to register. They couldn't find other jobs so they followed us around everywhere we went, walking with us as if they were bulletproof. They also spread rumors that the Freedom House was protected by armed men. We were all still a little up tight and afraid to sleep at night, but after a while, when the whites didn't come back, we figured the rumors worked. The threats didn't bother me as much now. I began to feel almost safe with those men around all the time. Their interest, courage, and concern gave all of us that extra lift we needed.

The Revolt of the
Black Athlete

Harry Edwards

Harry Edwards

Traditionally, athletics has been one of the main routes out of the ghetto for black youth. In the boxing ring, on the playing fields and basketball courts of colleges and universities, blacks have received recognition and status for their athletic abilities. In return, they were expected to show gratitude to the white athletic establishment for having taken them out of the poverty and deprivation of the slums. If it weren't for athletics, the argument goes, Willie Mays would still be on a plantation in Alabama. Bill Russell would be a janitor in Oakland, California. Harry Edwards would probably be in jail alongside his brother, serving twenty-five years to life for armed robbery.

The black athlete of an earlier generation had a public attitude of being grateful. Joe Louis was this kind of black athlete—humble, self-effacing, patriotic. Yet, being heavyweight champion of the world did not keep him from being treated like any other black. Joe Louis, however, did not protest.

The black college athlete of the sixties did. He knew that although he was cheered and hailed as a hero when he made a difficult catch, or a brilliant touchdown run, those cheers were not translated into equal treatment once he took off his uniform. In a simple change of dress, he went from hero to nigger. He was discriminated against in housing, jobs, in monies and favors given athletes, as well as being the everyday victim of the conscious and unconscious racism of the white students on campus.

Because of the Black Power movement, the black college athlete came to have a new pride in himself and his abilities. He recognized that he did as much for athletics as athletics did for him. No one was ultimately responsible for his athletic performances except himself. The coaches coached, but it was the athlete himself who had to have the discipline and commitment to make himself into the best in his area. As one professional football player put it when he was asked if football hadn't been "good" to him: "Hell, no! I've been good to it. Football did no better for me than what I put into it."

The feelings of black athletes remained practically unknown until a group of black track stars at California's San Jose State College announced that they were going to organize a black boycott of the 1968 Olympic Games to protest the treatment of black athletes, as well as black Americans.

The leader of the projected boycott was Harry Edwards, a 6' 8" basketball player and discus thrower who was an instructor in sociology at the school. Unfavorable criticism of the proposed boycott was international. But the athletic establishment, while forthrightly opposed to the boycott, was also frightened by it. Edwards was offered $100,000 to call it off. Former Vice President Hubert Humphrey and the late Senator Robert Kennedy appealed to him to reconsider. Edwards was unmoved.

The proposed boycott did not come off, but what resulted was perhaps even more effective. Tommie Smith and John Carlos were placed first and third respectively in the 200-meter dash at the Olympics. When they stood in the center of the field to receive their gold and bronze medals, and while the U.S. national anthem was being played, they lowered their heads and defiantly thrust their black-gloved fists into the air in the Black Power salute and held them there until the music died away.

White reaction in the United States would hardly have been greater if they had shot the President. But the photograph of their protest went around the world and became not only a symbol of the new black athlete, but a symbol for blacks everywhere. Smith and Carlos were suspended from the U.S. Olympic Team, but that mattered little. What mattered was that there was a new black athlete on the scene who demanded respect.

Harry Edwards's book, *The Revolt of the Black Athlete,* is not an autobiography as much as it is a history of blacks in athletics and the story of the events leading up to the protest at the 1968 Olympics. Yet, because he is an athlete, Edwards's story differs little from that of other black athletes. When he talks of what any black athlete has undergone, he is talking about himself. And when he talks of himself, he is talking for many blacks, athletes and non-athletes.

I am a college sociology teacher, age 25. Before I gave up games and went academic, I set a national junior college discus throw record of nearly 180 feet and track coaches fell all over me, as a likely internationalist. One Western coach called me (I'm 6-feet-8, 250 pounds), "a terrific animal"—without a moment's concern that I overheard his description.

But discus-tossing in no way dimmed my memory of the south side of East St. Louis, Illinois, where I grew up. Like everyone else, the Edwards family lived on beans and paste and watched neighbor kids freeze to death. We used an outhouse which finally collapsed in the hold and drank boiled drainage-ditch water.

Young mothers just *flew out* of the place. My own mother abandoned us when I was eight years old, later showing up with 86 stitches in her body after a street brawl. Cops jailed me for juvenile offenses. They jailed me when I was innocent. A brother of mine, today, serves 25-years-to-life in the Iowa State Penitentiary. Intelligent hearthside conversation didn't exist—intergroup allegiance and family discipline died under the weight of poverty.

I was the first boy from my area to graduate from high school. Until I was 17 I had never held a meaningful conversation with a white adult and until shortly before that I was unaware that one could vote in an election without first receiving pay—the $5 handed to a "block nigger" for his preempted ballot being a postulate of staying alive in East St. Louis.

One in tens of thousands of teen-agers has the muscle, speed, and coordination to "escape" such scenes—that is, physically leave the ghetto by signing with one of the universities which hotly recruit, buy, and ballyhoo Negro high school sport whizzes. And, once out of it and in a high-education environment, he's considered lucky. I was one of these.

Yet no medals I've won nor the B.A. and M.A. degrees which follow my name [and the Ph.D that is coming] can balance the East St. Louis I saw upon returning there last year. Jobs in trade unions, in public utilities, behind downtown store counters, remained blocked to 35,000 of the city's 105,000 population. Rags plugged paneless windows of tin shacks, children had been incinerated in fire-traps, riot had come and gone. A dungheap comatoseness still ruled six square miles.

"Are you still selling your vote for five bucks?" I asked the shot-to-hell young adults I grew up with.

"What else is it good for?" they replied.

If the weapons at their command aren't used in behalf of those left behind—it begins to occur to many athletes—how do they go on living with themselves? We have an avenue of power open to us: the most interracially significant gathering of peoples short of the U.N. If the most mobile minority in the public eye—Afro-American dashmen, leapers, musclemen, etc.—can arouse continuing worldwide publicity by not moving at all, at least the ditch-water drinkers will be remembered. Possibly the gain will be larger.

Until now, foreign interest in U.S. bigotry has been scattered and blurred, but when the Olympic Games walk-out first was announced, it rated Page One space in London, Paris, Tokyo, Rome. France's top sports periodical, *L'Equipe*, saw it as "the revolution incredible." The London *Daily Times'* Neil Allen wrote, "As we diagnose it, you are hitting at the middleclass America, the social force most perpetuating racism—telling it that no longer can sport be excluded from goals of assimilation." Japan's Sports Federation chief Tetsuo Ohba expressed surprise "at the depth of your racial problem," pointedly adding, "The Negro superstars made the Games worth seeing." As the national boycott leader, I have received dozens of *why?*-type inquiries from Europe, Asia, and Africa.

Focus of attention in this direction, abroad, actually began nearly two years ago when Muhammad Ali's world heavyweight title was lifted. U.S. black fight champs have been castrated before—in 1913, for instance, when Jack Johnson was forced into exile by white supremacists. Johnson was the classic, tragic loser. But the modern spotlight has caused the plight of one who believes that war is evil and who stuck with his belief to be well-noted.

Ali's treatment stunned black multitudes everywhere. To us, he was—is—a god. Demands that we appear in the Olympics, when placed alongside Ali's case, are revealed for what they are, especially when based on the pitch that our youngsters are missing the chance of a lifetime—the glory of being part of a world-championship show. Ali, as Cassius Clay, won an Olympic gold medal in 1960. Swell, baby. "Trust no Future, howe'er pleasant," as Longfellow said.

Another form of distortion of sportsmanship in which we are deeply involved is the class struggle heightened by Olympic medal-fever (outscore the Russians, show our superiority by use of complicated point tabulations). At the 1964 Tokyo-held games the U.S. won 20 gold medals in track-and-field, nine of them contributed by blacks. In Mexico City, without our help, vicarious patriotism no doubt will suffer. But what happens to the national point total concerns us not at all; we say, only, if Olympics zealots think white, then let them go to the starting line white.

If all our past heroes of the Games, their medals jangling, paraded into Washington, Detroit, or Cleveland, and confronted riot squads, all their speed wouldn't enable them to outrun bayonets and bullets. The sole factor separating a Tommie Smith, Ralph Boston, or John Carlos from becoming an ambushed Rev. Reeb or Medgar Evers is that they've been on no firing lines. Beyond the win-or-lose motivation there exists another intimate—and overlooked—concern of our membership.

Since the time of Jesse Owens it has been presumed that any poor but rugged youngster who was able to jump racial fences into a college haven was happy all day long. He—the All-American, the subsidized, semiprofessional racer—was fortunate. Mostly, this is a myth.

In 1960, for example, I was recruited by San Jose State College, a prominent "track school." Fine things were promised. "You'll be accepted here," the head coach and deans assured me. It developed that of 16 campus fraternities (as Greek in name as Plato, who revered the democracy of the Olympic Games) not one would pledge Harry Edwards (or anyone of color). The better restaurants were out of bounds and social activity was nil—I was invited nowhere outside "blood" circles.

Leaving California, I spent two years acquiring a Master's degree at Cornell University. Returning to San Jose State as a teacher, I knocked on door after door bearing "vacancy" signs, but Mr. Charley was so sorry—the rental room suddenly wasn't available. The end-up: a cold cement-floor garage, costing $75 a month.

Not long later I came to know Tommie Smith, whose 0:19.5 is the world 220-yard record and whom this same state college uses to impress and procure other speedsters and footballers of his race. "I have you beat," he said. "My wife's pregnant. We have no decent house. So far 13 lovely people have turned me down."

Much of the headbusting and police crackdowns at schools originate in Afro-American student frustration over housing, an area where valuable, "taken-care-of athletes" are thought to be uninvolved. Athletic Department p.r. men skillfully make this seem so. However, the great majority of black varsity men live, like Smith, in backstreet bed-in-the-wall pads located far from their classes, and overpriced. Existing as celebrity-pariahs, they go along with it because (1) they're dependent upon Charley's scholarship funding; (2) they're shy and tractable, taught early to "respect everyone, whether they respect you or not," or—"remember, as part of the Big Team you're safe from those Spookhunters outside"; (3) if they openly rebelled, back to pushing a poolhall broom they'd go.

The answer was expressed some weeks ago by Lee Evans, a collegian who ranks as the world's second-best quarter-miler of all time. "That bag," he says, "is rapidly changing. We're all through having our insides churned just when we think we're emancipated."

The examples are many and they vary little: in 1967, Southern California U's great footballer-trackman, O. J. Simpson, was worth at least $500,000 to USC at the box-office. Many awards followed. Simpson, should he desire, could not become a member of more than 90 per cent of the groups which honored him with banquets and trophies. [Typical are the many restricted athletic clubs and country clubs throughout the nation.] Such organizations, however, feel quite justified in using Simpson's name to enhance their own identification with athletics.

At Southern Methodist University last year, "one-man-team" halfback Jerry Levias drew so many death threats and so much abuse by mail and phone that he was given a bodyguard and begged by his family to quit sports. Varsity Negroes at the University of Washington, excluded from organized dances, golf, and ski-trips, boycotted the school's sports program. At UCLA a public-relations gag was put on 7-ft.-1 Lew Alcindor; he shook it off to reveal that he's been niggerblasted by fans, cold-shouldered by students, and told to get lost.

In Kansas City, former Heisman Trophy-winner-turned-pro Mike Garrett found a bachelor apartment unobtainable and exploded in print. "Troublemaker" the local community said of him.

In sections of the Bible Belt and in Southern states where many Olympic point-winners are developed, trackmen routinely break records, but their friends must sit far from the finish line in segregated seats.

At a recent Los Angeles Boycott Olympics Project conference, word arrived that Dickie Howard had been found dead, not far away, of an overdose of drugs. Howard was a fairly good student and he won an Olympic 400-meter bronze medal at Rome in 1960. Finding too many doors shut, he disintegrated and at 29 took his own life.

Post-Olympic careers for black grads in coaching,

teaching, advertising, and business are so few (a Bob Hayes in pro football, a Rafer Johnson in radio, a Hayes Jones in recreation direction, are but tokens in the overall picture) that the following happened: a college alumnus famous for his accomplishments as an Olympic athlete approached a TV agency. As he well knew, the endorsement, testimonial, and product-pushing industry generally employs as many of his kind as you'll find swimming in pools in Southampton. However, he had a winning smile. To his suggestion that he could sell breakfast food or toothpaste, network executives said, "Use you on commercials? Not hardly. We'd lose 60 per cent of our audience. But we do have a job open." He promptly was handed a card to be held up before studio audiences, reading—"Laugh."

Not laughing himself, he held it up. No other work was open to him.

As much as Olympic officials denounce the profit motive and try to legislate it away, most athletes waste no time in cashing in on their reputations. The Games and commercialism are so closely tied that no longer is it arguable that they are not. One big goal is a job with a school. What major universities employ a black athletic director, head coach, assistant coach, or even a head scout? Answer: almost none. Equipment-man and bus-driving positions are open, always, in number.

Once upon a time, children, we inform men who

are undecided about joining the boycott and come to us torn between their personal need and a larger need, there was Binga Dismond. He's forgotten now. Binga was the original Negro track sensation in America—a meteor who flared in Chicago in 1916–17, long before the Eddie Tolans, Ralph Metcalfes, and De-Hart Hubbards. "Binga," wrote Charley Paddock, the Caucasian sprint champion of that time, "could beat any man alive at 440 yards. But he was required to run on the outside of the pack, all the way around, so as to avoid physical contact with any white. Eventually, discouraged, he disappeared."

From "Long Way" Dismond we move to the subject of Jesse Owens: "immortal" Jesse, whose four gold medals won at the 1936 Olympics in Berlin left Hitler much discomfited. For 30 years Olympic Committee and Amateur Athletic Union officials have used Owens as the prime illustration of how pride and hope of a minority can be uplifted through the feats of a blood brother. The recorded facts—not mentioned —are:

The "Buckeye Bullet" finished his amazing Reich Sportsfield appearances on a Sunday. Within 12 hours he was put aboard a train to Cologne and sent on a grueling European trip by his promoters, the AAU. In the next 10 days, Owens raced eight times and lost 14 pounds. Exhausted, he was ordered to Sweden for still more exhibitions. All gate receipts would accrue to the Swedes and the AAU. Owens refused to go. Within weeks, he was suspended by the AAU and thrown out of amateur sports, for life.

When Owens next raced it was for money against horses and motorcycles in sleazy hippodromes in Mexico and Reno. Over ensuing years a modicum of advantages have come Jesse Owens' way; but to friends he says, "I've never been in the mainstream. They won't put me on any key Olympic committees, the policy groups. I've been used."

None of the organizers of Boycott Olympics was surprised when Owens, last November, expressed sympathy with our motives, but found boycott over-severe—a "wrong approach" to the problem. For he belongs to a controlled generation, the inheritors of Binga Dismond running on the outside.

Does it occur to Jesse Owens that blacks are ineligible by color-line and by endless economic obstacles to compete in some 80 per cent of scheduled Olympic events? Rowing, skating, swimming, shooting, horsebacking, yachting, skiing, fencing, gymnastics, modern pentathlon, water polo, among others, are activities outside our cultural reach, although wasn't it Baron Pierre de Coubertin, the French scholar and humanist, who inspired the revival of the Olympics in 1896, who wrote, "The important thing in the Games is not winning, but taking part"? And who inscribed, "The foundation of human morality lies in mutual respect—and to respect one another, it is necessary to know one another."

"Know" requires association, yes? Nineteen Olympiads later, no black ever has been a member of the American Olympic Committee's governing board, nor held a responsible post on any of the multiple individual sport federations. When we demand a place, back comes the disguised echo—of Maddox, Barnett, Wallace, Bull Connor.

Concededly, poor whites aren't yachtsmen, equestrians or badge-wearers, either. But as United States District Court Judge Wade H. McCree of Detroit remarked, "No one in this country is poor or outside because he's white." I'm sure Jesse Owens grasps the whole Olympic picture, agrees deep-down with us and would move to our support but for the bonds forged long ago.

Humble is out now. Action that is non-action is in. Quadrennially, the newspapers exclaim over feats of the Ralph Bostons, Bob Hayses, and Henry Carrs—record-breakers. Olympic symbols.

Symbolically, they can only serve a wrong purpose. Overseas audiences hear little of bloodshed in the human-rights struggle. But when the Asian, Nordic, or Slav sees a white Richmond Flowers of Tennessee passing a relay baton to a Charles Greene or an O. J. Simpson they deduce, "Those boys, indeed, are equal." Greene or Simpson, of course, couldn't race on many southern U.S. tracks or join a fraternity or a down-town A.C. in the North, any more than Thurgood Marshall, of our highest courts, could be named a county attorney in Alabama.

On the Olympic Committee for Human Rights, we think simply. We believe that the answer to why Afro-Americans are relegated to a subhuman sphere is one of two—either they want to be classed that way or society feels that they should be there. The first reason is obviously ludicrous. Application of the second of the two answers has led the Union to the edge of ultimate revolution.

If the fastest among us can show that our sense of personal worth and obligation outweighs any re-wards offered us and that we represent the many, something may be accomplished. The aim of Pierre de Coubertin may be recognized more than 70 years later.

G.I. in Vietnam

David Parks

David Parks

In every war in which America has engaged, blacks have been willing soliders. During the Revolutionary War, blacks fought at Bunker Hill, Yorktown, and every other famous battle site. Blacks crossed the Delaware with Washington and when Paul Revere rode through the streets yelling "The British are coming!" he woke up black Minutemen as well as white.

Blacks fought and died in the War of 1812. They fought with Andrew Jackson at the Battle of New Orleans, and Jackson afterward maintained that the city would have been lost except for the black troops. They fought in the Civil War, and after that war there were black cavalry regiments who fought Indians in the West. Black soldiers ran up San Juan Hill ahead of Theodore Roosevelt's Rough Riders in the Spanish-American War and were highly praised by him afterwards. World War I, World War II, the Korean War, and the war in Vietnam all saw the participation in great numbers of black soldiers, who—almost without exception—fought well, fought hard, and fought long.

Yet blacks have always participated in America's wars with mixed feelings. At home they were discriminated against. To many it seemed contradictory that they should fight and risk their lives to insure the freedom of a country that allowed them no freedom. But they also thought that if they proved themselves willing to defend such a country, it would be more difficult for that country to continue to discriminate against blacks. How could America refuse to extend all the rights and privileges of citizenship to a people who fought for the country?

With the war in Vietnam, the thinking of many young black men changed. David Parks was one of them. The son of a distinguished black writer-photographer-composer, Gordon Parks, David grew up differently from most blacks. His father was famous and affluent. David knew no poverty and hardly any discrimination. When he was drafted at the age of twenty-one, he went without the slightest hesitation. He was aware that there were many blacks who were calling the war in Vietnam a "white man's war." He knew that blacks had been shot down in the streets of American cities by policemen and National Guardsmen during the urban rebellions. But he went, because he was an American and believed in America.

His two-year tour of duty in Vietnam changed the way David looked at himself and America. On the battlefields of Vietnam, fighting alongside white soldiers, he learned about racism and discrimination. It was everywhere, even in the very fact of the war itself.

David kept a diary of his Army life. When he was discharged from the service in 1967, at the suggestion of his father he used the diary as the basis for a short, intense book. *GI Diary* was published the following year.

In the selection reprinted here, David describes the treatment he and other black soldiers suffered at the hands of white soldiers and officers and his reactions to it. It seems ironic that it was while he was fighting for the alleged freedom of the South Vietnamese that he learned just how little freedom he himself had.

———————◆———————

January 31, 1967

The FO's* job is one of the hairiest in a mortar platoon. He's on more patrols because an FO is required to be with the patrolling squad at all times, and there are only three FOs to cover sixteen squads. The odds are against him. Sgt. Paulson hand-picks the men for this job. So far he's fingered only Negroes and Puerto Ricans. I think he's trying to tell us something. I do know he gives me a sour look every time he sees me at the FDC† controls. Every time he comes around I get a feeling that I should have been born white. It's a bitch. If only the souls and Puerto Ricans could tell the world what really happens to them in this man's army. We do receive more than our share of the shit.

* Forward Observer
† Fire Direction Control

The biggest laugh I've had lately was when I was on radio watch the other night and Paulson thought he'd sneak up on the radio tent and catch me napping. I heard a grunt and thud and looked out to see Paulson spread-eagled on the ground. I knew just what he'd been up to and burst out laughing. I really cracked up. Paulson was so ticked off all he did was get up and walk away. Paulson is a real ass. He's always telling me that Negroes are lazy and won't help themselves, etc. I tell him he's full of shit and end up filling sandbags.

Whitey is the same throughout this whole damn organization. Somehow I thought it would be different this time. Especially over here, where survival is the thing. But that seems to cut no ice with Mister Pale. All the souls in the platoon are beginning to gripe, but not enough as far as I'm concerned. Lt. Alden, the platoon leader, usually calls us Negroes "you people." Zerman, a Jewish cat from New York, is hip to what is happening, but he's got his own problems. Sgt. Golas changes with the weather. Sometimes he's human. At other times he treats us souls like we are dirt. What the hell. Maybe it's the pressure.

Ten more months of this crap. These guys bug me more than Charlie. I'm learning one hell of a lesson in here. Whitey's a good teacher.

February 7, 1967

The handwriting is definitely on the wall. Paulson says I'm not figuring the FDC data fast enough. Getting my walking boots ready.

February 9, 1967

Just got kicked out of my beautiful FDC job. The good Sgt. Paulson strikes again. He gave me the news with a smile. I am now Forward Observer Parks, attached to the First Platoon command track. On mission our platoon has to dismount and go after Charlie on foot. And I'm carrying that fucking telephone with the antenna, which makes a beautiful target. It's a sergeant's job, but Paulson's not going to promote me. The bastard.

May 25, 1967

Rain has brought everything to a standstill, and Bravo is under about ten feet of water. Sometimes I would prefer action to sitting around listening to these officers beat their gums. It's either how many battles they've won or how many broads they've laid. At times they act like children the way they demand attention. And you'd better jump if you don't want your ass out on that firing line. The only way to keep cool with them is to lie quiet. Show the slightest sign of intelligence and you've had it. Especially if you're a Negro. Pratt and Gurney are pretty bright souls. But every time you see them they are pulling a shit detail while the white cats lie in their bunks enjoying life. A couple of the white guys got so ashamed that they came to the old man today and complained about Pratt and Gurney getting all the shit. I hope it does some good, but I doubt it.

Sgt. Paulson is detail boss. Capt. Thomas is a good officer and most of the time he treats me OK, probably because I'm his RTO.* But sometimes he forgets himself. I made the mistake of showing him a clipping Deedee sent about Martin Luther King's denouncing the war. "Who the hell does he think he is? Just because he got a Nobel Prize he thinks he can run the fucking world." He went on, ripping King apart. I said that I thought Dr. King was a man who believed in justice for all people. Then I shut my big mouth. I wasn't in the mood for a night patrol.

June 6, 1967

Wow! Got a letter from Ken Gillman today. Liz told him I've been accepted at RIT. Hope it's true.

* Radio-Telephone Operator

Why doesn't Pops write?

For the past ten days we have been operating in the Tan An area, just south of Saigon. We got two kills the other day that will be hard to forget. The choppers spotted them as they were trying to get away, and their gunners riddled them. We finished them off with the 50s. It was just bloody raw meat mixed with mud. Not a very pretty picture. Passmore, the other RTO, got sick and let go on the old man's boots. He still isn't used to it after six months. I didn't get sick. But I didn't want any steak dinner after that either.

June 8, 1967

Well, it's true. I've been accepted. Got the letters from RIT and Pops this afternoon. This should push me out eighty days earlier. Can't wait. Damned tired of living in dirt, taking orders and being called names by my superiors. Paulson insults the Negro soldiers just for kicks, I'm sure. Pratt hates his guts. "I'm going to mistake that son-of-a-bitch for Charlie one of these days, baby," he said, after pulling patrol for the third straight night.

I've got 250 missions under my belt and over 25 major operations. That's good enough for a full tour already. But the scuttlebutt is that we're headed for the DMZ. Hope not. Could be true. We've killed a lot of VC around the Delta region. We have a good fighting record. Some of the villagers have come to think of us as murderers of civilians. That's one of the main tragedies of war, so many innocent people getting hurt or killed. Some of the guys have indulged in some raping too. They even brag about it.

Jones, a Negro guy who joined us recently, killed a civilian the other day, and in front of his three kids. We'd taken the civilian into custody because he didn't have an identification card.* We put him in a hut, together with his wife and kids, while we waited for the local police to come and identify him. The man tried to get out of the hut a couple of times, but each time Jones ordered him back. Jones and I chewed the fat for a while, then I went outside and sat against the wall of the hut for a nap. Suddenly an M-16 went off, so close I thought I'd been hit. I rushed back to see Jones standing over the guy, who was trying to get to his feet. Blood was pumping out of his back like a fountain. Jones just stood there sweating and shaking. He said the guy ran for the door and he had to shoot. The kids were crying and holding on to one another, and his wife was kneeling over him, kind of moaning. A medic came and tried to save the guy, but he was gone. I could tell by the way the medic

---

* All Vietnamese civilians carry an identification card issued by the Government of the Republic of Vietnam.

shook his head from side to side. A little later the local police arrived and said that the man was clean—he wasn't a VC. Too bad they didn't arrive a little earlier.

That night the wife complained to the Vietnamese authorities, because the next morning an MP came out to investigate. The CO told Jones not to worry, that he was just doing his job.

I still don't know what made that guy try to get out of the hut. The awful thing is that if we had tied him up as we should have he wouldn't have tried to escape, and then he wouldn't have gotten shot. The only reason we didn't tie him up was because his family was there and we thought it would make them feel bad. I can't stop thinking about those kids. They'll hate us for the rest of their lives. And who can blame them?

July 24, 1967

A strange change has come over the CO. He's suddenly begun to think of himself as the great killer of men, brags about it and laughs about the Charlies he has killed. I've always respected him more than most of the other officers, and when he's under pressure I try to help him. Sometimes he's buddy-buddy, but other times he treats me like a flunky. A couple of weeks ago we were sitting around in a rice paddy waiting for orders and the old man decided to get in some practice with his 45. He had me sloshing around in the mud setting up C-ration cans as targets for half an hour, like a pin boy. And the other day he dropped his rifle in the muck and asked me to pick it up. I knew he was expecting me to clean it off, but I just handed it to him and walked off. He was really pissed. Passmore's his boy for that kind of thing. I think he ended up by cleaning the rifle, too. I've been through too much shit to take any from Thomas at this point.

Just received the operation order for tomorrow's mission. It will be a three-day mission, and my twenty-third airmobile lift. The monsoons are still with us. I miss our tracks.

August 1, 1967

On Operation Lansing to clear Highway 4 from the Delta to the capital.

Charlie woke us up at 2 A.M. a couple of mornings ago and we have been catching hell ever since. We were to go out on operation against him in a few hours, but he caught us off guard. He threw rocket and mortar fire at us and everything else he had in his arsenal. We scrambled around in the darkness grabbing things we needed to survive or kill with. We

132

finally got onto our tracks and were moving out of base camp when I suddenly realized that this was my last operation. I thought about Harris, Gurney and all the other short-timers. And I began praying I'd make it. I kept praying as we headed for the battle zone where the VC had fired from. And I kept counting the operations and missions I had been on over and over, trying like hell to keep my cool.

We had already called the choppers in when the landing zone unit called saying they were being hit. Thomas gave the word, and we dismounted and moved over to help them. Then bullets started coming from every direction, even from friendly positions. We crawled as we fired, to keep out of the way of our own support. And I was awful thankful for all that crawling they put us through back at Riley. By now the landing zone unit was in bad trouble and Thomas took us on a short cut through the swamp. Muck was waist-deep, but we kept firing as we went.

Then suddenly I was stuck, sinking in. Each time I tried to pull out I went in deeper. The other guys were leaving me behind, going ahead blasting into the wood line. It was useless to yell for help. No one could have heard me in the noise. The VC was still pouring it into us. Suddenly I felt tired, so tired I wasn't scared any more. I suppose I was giving up. Short-time had caught up with me. Then someone came splashing past. It was that bastard Sgt. Paulson. Now he looked like an angel as he extended his rifle, butt first, and hauled me out of that hole. We both kept on moving forward.

By dawn we had the VC surrounded, but they wouldn't give in. There are over two thousand of them in the area and they fought all day. They tried to break through by pounding Charlie Company that evening. A Med Evac chopper had been shot down in the Charlie Company area and ten guys died trying to secure it. The VC knew that this was the weak spot to try to get through, but our artillery wouldn't let them. We listened to the artillery rounds pounding the VC escape route all last night.

Charlie broke through at one point, but he couldn't escape. We're still on his tail. But he knows this country well, and there are plenty of places for him to hide. Right now things have quieted down. The army's set up showers in a little town nearby and all the guys have gone. I'm on radio watch in the track.

September 9, 1967

I take off for home day after tomorrow. Yowie!

Just got back from Bravo. The guys were out on the wood line patrolling, so I didn't see them. Several guys got it while I was on R and R.* Don't know exactly who they are. Did see Passmore, who is being

---

* Rest and Relaxation

transferred to headquarters company. I never liked that guy, but when he walked me to the chopper that was taking me out, I couldn't help feeling some kinship with him. We've been through a lot together. I wished him the best and meant it. He said he hoped he'd see me on the other side and didn't mean it. I could do without that anyway.

The chopper ride back to Zulu is probably the last one I take in Nam. Looking down over the rice paddies I knew so well made me wonder if I had a right to be there. When I came into the army I had no questions, but I am leaving with some. Back in basic they told us over and over again that these people needed help, that they were poor and don't know how to solve their own problems, that we promised them our help, and that we couldn't go back on them. Well, there were times when it seemed we were doing them more harm than good.

I never felt that I was fighting for any particular cause. I fought to stay alive, and I killed to keep from being killed. Now that it's all over there is a funny feeling running through my stomach, when I think of what could have happened to me. When you're in the middle of the fighting, you become strong and do things you didn't think possible. You only think about it afterward. It's hard for me to believe I'm all here and in one piece. Somebody up there is with me after all.

September 11, 1967

Well, we're on a good old TWA plane heading for the States. All the guys are just sitting and smiling at one another, thankful to be aboard. And all I can think about is that I'm safe. I tried to pick out some of the areas we fought in down there, but it was hazy and we were climbing too fast. Nam is really such a small country. Many of the guys down there won't make this trip sitting upright. The officers are smiling at us. They are fly-boys. Probably seen as much action as we have. But they haven't lived in the mud with the enemy like we have.

6:30 P.M.

Just left Okinawa, where we fueled up. A lot of our guys got it down there in the last war.

September 12, 1967
11:30 A.M.

Taking off from Honolulu. Should be in San Francisco around chow time.

136

4:20 P.M.

Just spotted the California coastline. Just forty-eight hours and I'll be out of this man's army.

September 13, 1967

Homeward bound. Went across on the thirteenth and going home on the thirteenth. Must be my lucky number. The white guy who sold me my ticket at the airport gave me some really dirty looks. He pitched my ticket at me like I was dirt. There is nothing like the army to make you conscious of such things. The ticket seller reminded me of how some of my white officers treated me. Well, I'm a Negro and I'm back home where color makes the difference. I was feeling good on that plane from Namsville. Thought I'd left all my problems behind. Hell, the new ones will just have to wait. I'm going to enjoy myself for a few days —just knowing Charlie won't be around to wake me up in the morning.

BIBLIOGRAPHY

The books from which the episodes in this anthology were taken are available in the following editions.

Narrative of the Life of Frederick Douglass, an American Slave written by himself.

> Hardcover: Belknap Press, Harvard University Press.
> H. C. Publishers, Inc.
> Paperback: Belknap Press, Harvard University Press.
> Dolphin Books, Doubleday & Company, Inc.
> Signet Books, New American Library, Inc.

Black Boy by Richard Wright.

> Hardcover: Harper & Row, Publishers.
> Paperback: Perennial Classics, Harper & Row.

The Long Shadow of Little Rock by Daisy Bates.

> Hardcover: David McKay Company, Inc.

The Autobiography of Malcolm X by Malcolm X with the assistance of Alex Haley.

> Hardcover: Grove Press, Inc.
> Paperback: Grove Press, Inc.

Off My Chest by Jimmy Brown with Myron Cope.

> Hardcover: Doubleday & Company, Inc.

Coming of Age in Mississippi by Anne Moody.

> Hardcover: The Dial Press, Inc.
> Paperback: Dell Publishing Company, Inc.

The Revolt of the Black Athlete by Harry Edwards.

> Hardcover: The Free Press.

GI Diary by David Parks.

> Hardcover: Harper & Row, Publishers.

RAE PACE ALEXANDER *was born in Phila-delphia and educated at Boston University and at Bank Street College of Education, New York. She has pre-viously compiled an annotated bibliography of black and bi-racial children's books for the N.A.A.C.P. Her article, "Rigorous Appraisal of Bi-Racial Children's Books," was published by the Council on Interracial Books for Children, Inc. Miss Alexander is at present a candidate for a doctoral degree at Teachers College, Columbia University.*

JULIUS LESTER *was born in St. Louis, Missouri, grew up in Nashville, Tennessee, was graduated from Fisk University, and now lives in New York City with his wife and two children. A frequent reviewer for the* New York Times Book Review *and contributor to national periodicals, Mr. Lester has three adult books, two juveniles, and two record albums to his name. His book* To Be a Slave *was runner-up for the Newbery Prize. He has a regular radio program on WBAI and also teaches at the New School for Social Research.*

DATE DUE

DEC 7 1974			
	Withdrawn From		
	Ohio Northern		
	University Library		
GAYLORD			PRINTED IN U.S.A.